2/13

SUPPORTING CREATIVE EXCELLENCE

ADC

• SINCE 1920 •

Keep fighting the good fight.

EDITOR
Jennifer Larkin Kuzler

EDITORIAL ASSISTANTS
Meredith Feir
Kim Hanzich

AWARDS STAFF
Ariel Adkins
Carol Arango
Scott Ballum
Meredith Feir
Jennifer Griffiths
Kim Hanzich
Colin McCullough
Chelsea Temkin
Michael Waka

COPY EDITOR
Elizabeth A. McCaffrey

2012 CALL FOR ENTRIES,
GALA INVITATION,
& ANNUAL DESIGN
Agency: DDB New York
Chief Creative Officer:
Matt Eastwood
Executive Creative Director:
Menno Kluin
Art Director: Carlos Wigle
Copywriter: Aron Fried
Designers/Typographers:
Juan Carlos Pagan,
Brian Gartside,
Joanne O'Neill
Illustrator: Rami Niemi
Art Producers:
Carol Brandwein, Jane Piampiano

BOOK PRODUCTION
Nathaniel Salgueiro

PUBLISHED IN
ASSOCIATION WITH
AVA Publishing SA
Rue des Fontenailles 16
1000 Lausanne 6
Switzerland
Tel : +41 78 600 5109
enquiries@avabooks.com

DISTRIBUTED IN USA & CANADA BY
Ingram Publishers Services Inc.
1 Ingram Blvd
La Vergne TN 37086
Tel: +1 866 400 5351
customer.services@
ingrampublisherservices.com

DISTRIBUTED
EX-NORTH AMERICA BY
Thames & Hudson
181a High Holborn
London WC1V 7QX
United Kingdom
Tel: +4420 7845 50000
sales@thameshudson.co.uk

PRODUCTION BY
AVA Book Production
Pte. Ltd., Singapore
Tel: +65 6334 8173
Email: production
@avabooks.com.sg
Library of Congress
Cataloging-in-
Publication Data
Art Directors Club
(New York, N.Y.).
The Art Directors Club Annual/
Art Directors Club
(New York, N.Y.). p. cm.
Includes index.
ISBN: 9782940496211
eISBN: 9782940447527
(pbk. : alk. paper)
1. Commercial art—
Exhibitions.
2. Art Directors Club
(New York, N.Y.)
—Exhibitions.
NC997.A1 A69

The Art Directors Annual honors the year's best work in design and advertising around the globe through print, photography, illustration, broadcast and interactive media. This edition also proudly presents the most recent class of Hall of Fame laureates.

THE ART DIRECTORS CLUB
106 West 29th Street
New York, NY 10001
United States of America
www.adcglobal.org

ISBN: 9782940496211

Hall of Fame
Designism
Design
Illustration
Photography
Motion
Integrated
Interactive
Advertising
Student

Contents

Benjamin Palmer
ADC Board President

Welcome to the 91st Annual of the Art Directors Club! This is my first year as Board President, and so far it has been amazing. We are in an exciting time in the industry. There is a lot of change afoot and the ADC is right in the middle of it – with a new Executive Director, tons of newly introduced programs, and lots of opportunities to interact with the Club and other members.

It is a testament to the enduring need for the ADC that ninety-one years in, the organization still plays an integral role in the creative industry. We work to fulfill a lot of missions here at the Club, but fundamentally, our central goal is to bring our peers closer together. Times of change provide important opportunities for inspiration and growth – we can celebrate the best work, but that can't be fully effective without an equal measure of education and forward thinking about what is coming next. I hope you enjoy the work in this Annual, and I hope to see you all soon at the ADC Gallery.

Ignacio Oreamuno
ADC Executive Director

No advertising and design organization has witnessed more change in the industry than the ADC. In eight years, we are going to celebrate our 100th anniversary, and I predict that these next eight years hold more unexpected and drastic changes than all the ones to date combined.

Like the circles inside a tree that reveal its age, the Annuals of the ADC are a good way to measure the longevity and history of our industry. The rise of television clearly marked the beginning of a new phase in our industry and the Annuals reflect that. Soon after, the web came, making the interactive experience hard to explain and bring to life in our annuals. Nowadays, it's hard to make a clear distinction between interactive, digital, social and traditional. I predict that annuals will soon cease to exist in their current form, and that is not a bad thing. Things change and as creative professionals we should love and embrace, not fear, this change.

I'm proud to have been brought in to lead the biggest transformation the ADC has ever experienced. We are not just going to adapt, but instead we are going to throw ourselves head first into the uncertainty of the future to serve the industry as a guiding light. This year will mark the biggest ever international expansion through ADC programs like Portfolio Night and the Tomorrow Awards. In addition to that we are going to expand the value we offer drastically, creating higher quality events and perks of all kinds to better serve our members. I believe the best years of the ADC are yet to come, and we are going to do everything in our power to make this happen.

As we at the ADC make that happen, I reach out and open the door to the ADC to you, our members, because the ADC belongs to you.

Making it into the Hall of Fame is tougher than ever.

Keep fighting the good fight.

ArtDirectorsClub

Hall Of Fame

In the four decades since it was established, the Art Directors Club Hall of Fame has become synonymous with excellence in visual communication. Its inductees represent a staggeringly wide-ranging set of creative endeavors, and with each year the scope of their accomplishments continues to expand. This was all by design. When the Hall of Fame was inaugurated by the ADC Board of Directors in 1971, it was understood that true achievement defies convention and pushes boundaries. That year's Annual states that those honorees "and the people that will follow in the Hall of Fame, have lived their lives as art directors, salesmen, thinkers, innovators, but most of all, artists." We are proud to recognize five individuals who, each in their own way, fully live up to that title.

Anthony P. Rhodes & Louise Fili

Co-Chairs, 2012 Hall of Fame Selection Committee

Hall of Fame
Selection Committee

Anthony P. Rhodes
Executive Vice President,
School of Visual Arts
Hall of Fame Co-Chair

Louise Fili
President,
Louise Fili Ltd
Hall of Fame Co-Chair

Bob Giraldi
Film Director and Owner,
Giraldi Media
Chair, SVA Live Action
Short Film Graduate Department

Doug Jaeger
Partner,
JaegerSloan, Inc.
ADC Second Vice President
ADC Advisory Board President

Gail Anderson
Faculty,
School of Visual Arts

George Lois
Art Director
ADC Past President

Janet Froelich
Creative Director,
Real Simple Magazine
ADC Board Member

Benjamin Palmer
Co-Founder and CEO,
The Barbarian Group
ADC Board President

Ivan Chermayeff
Founding Partner,
Chermayeff & Geismar

Richard Wilde
Chair, Design and
Advertising Department,
School of Visual Arts
ADC Past President

Barry Blitt

Barry Blitt is a cartoonist and illustrator, who through his many *New Yorker* covers, has become one of the pre-eminent American satirists. He is probably best known for "The Politics of Fear," his provocative July 2008 image of Michelle and Barack Obama, dressed as a Muslim and a militant with an AK-47, fist-bumping in the Oval Office.

Since 1992, Blitt has contributed 250 illustrations and 70 covers to *The New Yorker*. His most celebrated covers include "Deluged," (George Bush's White House awash in the aftermath of Katrina) — it was voted Cover of the Year by the American Society of Magazine Editors in 2006. Many of his other *New Yorker* covers have also been finalists for the same award including, in 2008, "Narrow Stance" (a frontal view of the Iranian president being solicited in a public bathroom) and "I'll Get It!" (Hillary Clinton and Barack Obama in bed, both reaching for the red phone ringing at 3AM), "First Anniversary" (Obama walking on water) in 2010 and "The Book of Life" (Steve Jobs waiting at the pearly gates) in 2012.

Blitt's work also appears in publications such as *Entertainment Weekly*, *TIME* Magazine, *Vanity Fair*, *Rolling Stone* and *The Atlantic*. He illustrated Frank Rich's weekly column in *The New York Times* for seven years. He has been honored with exhibitions and awards from the Society of Illustrators, *Print* and *American Illustration* among many others.

In 1994, Blitt illustrated a postage stamp for Canada Post. He designed an animated sequence for an episode of *Saturday Night Live* in 1996.

Blitt has illustrated many children's books, among them *The 39 Apartments of Ludwig van Beethoven*, *Once Upon a Time, the End (Asleep in 60 Seconds)* and *George Washington's Birthday: A Mostly True Tale*, published by Random House this past winter.

Unfazed by the Digital Age, Blitt never stopped drawing with a dip pen and watercolors. When he isn't drawing, he plays the piano, occasionally performing at the Society of Illustrators with "The Half-Tones," an illustrators jazz group he founded with Joe Ciardiello and Michael Sloan. A Canadian national born in 1958, Blitt grew up in Côte Saint-Luc, Quebec, a municipality on the Island of Montreal. He currently resides in Connecticut.

Jan. 10, 1994   THE NEW YORKER   Price $2.50

David Droga

Growing up in an Australian ski resort, David couldn't imagine anything better than touring the world as a ski instructor. Ironically, it was his imagination that took him abroad, not his skis.

David launched his career by winning top student honors at the Australian Writers & Art Directors School.

At 22, he became a partner and Executive Creative Director of OMON Sydney. Over the next five years, OMON won Australian Agency of the Year twice and Ad of the Year four times.

In 1996, David moved to Singapore to become Executive Creative Director of Saatchi & Saatchi Singapore and Regional Creative Director of Saatchi Asia.

By 1998, Saatchi was the region's most successful network, and Saatchi & Saatchi Singapore was at the epicenter of this transformation *Media Marketing* named Saatchi Asia Regional Network of the Year and *Advertising Age* named the Singapore office International Agency of the Year.

Then, the Saatchi head office came calling. At 29, David was promoted to Executive Creative Director of Saatchi & Saatchi London.

In 2002, Saatchi & Saatchi London won Agency of the Year at the Cannes International Advertising Festival. Later that year, both *Advertising Age* and *Adweek* named Saatchi Agency of the Year.

In 2003, another challenge came knocking and David packed his bags again. This time, he headed to New York City as the first-ever Worldwide Chief Creative Officer of the Publicis Network. In less than two years, Publicis enjoyed a very public creative and new business renaissance around the world.

However, tired of growing other people's companies, David decided to start his own agency.

In 2006, Droga5 was launched in New York City.

Droga5 has twice been named Agency of the Year by *Creativity* magazine (2007 and 2011), and made *Advertising Age*'s Agency A-List in both 2010 and 2011. It is now the fastest-growing independent agency in the United States of America.

Along the way, David has also received countless personal accolades. To date, he is the single-most-awarded creative at the Cannes International Advertising Festival, with over 70 Cannes Lions, including six Grand Prix and four Titanium lions.

In 2005, David was inducted into the American Advertising Federation Hall of Achievement. *Esquire* magazine has featured David in its annual "Best and Brightest" issue three times, and he was the first recipient of the *Boards* magazine Lifetime Achievement Award. In 2012, the American Australian Association and G'Day USA honored him for his business success and he received the overall Advance Global Australian Award. While in London, he was nominated Best Creative Director in the UK's Best of the Best Awards and named World's Best Creative Director by *Advertising Age*.

From his time in Asia, David is included in *Media Marketing*'s Hall of Fame and was honored with a Lifetime Achievement Award by *Campaign Brief Asia*.

In Australia, *Creative* magazine named him Australian Creative Person of the Decade.

David sits on the board of New York's New Museum, and lives with his wife and three children in Manhattan.

Beyond his family and building a new venture, David's favorite topics are art, the environment and anything Australian.

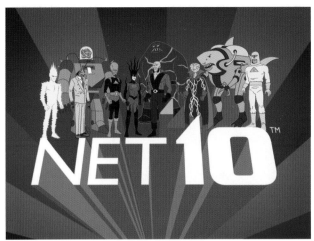

Mary Ellen Mark

Mary Ellen Mark has achieved worldwide visibility through her numerous books, exhibitions and editorial magazine work. She is a contributing photographer to *The New Yorker* and has published photo essays and portraits in such publications as *LIFE*, *The New York Times* Magazine, *Rolling Stone* and *Vanity Fair*. For over four decades, she has traveled extensively to make pictures that reflect a high degree of humanism. Today, she is recognized as one of our most respected and influential photographers. Her images of our world's diverse cultures have become landmarks in the field of documentary photography. Her portrayals of Mother Teresa, Indian circuses - and brothels in Bombay were the product of many years of work in India. A photo essay on runaway children in Seattle became the basis of the Academy Award-nominated film *Streetwise*, directed and photographed by her husband, Martin Bell.

Mary Ellen was presented with the Cornell Capa Award by the International Center of Photography in 2001. She has also received the Infinity Award for Journalism, an Erna & Victor Hasselblad Foundation Grant and a Walter Annenberg Grant for her book and exhibition project on *America*. Among her other awards are the John Simon Guggenheim Fellowship, the Matrix Award for Outstanding Woman in the Field of Film/Photography and the Dr. Erich Salomon Award for Outstanding Merits in the Field of Journalistic Photography. She was also presented with honorary Doctor of Fine Arts degrees from her alma mater, the University of Pennsylvania and the University of the Arts; three fellowships from the National Endowment for the Arts; the Photographer of the Year Award from the Friends of Photography; the World Press Award for Outstanding Body of Work Throughout the Years; the Victor Hasselblad Cover Award; two Robert F. Kennedy Awards; and the Creative Arts Award Citation for Photography at Brandeis University.

She has published 17 books including *Passport* (Lustrum Press, 1974), *Ward 81* (Simon & Schuster, 1979), *Falkland Road* (Knopf, 1981), *Mother Teresa's Mission of Charity in Calcutta* (Friends of Photography, 1985),

The Photo Essay: Photographers at Work (A Smithsonian series), Streetwise (second printing, Aperture, 1992), Mary Ellen Mark: 25 Years (Bulfinch, 1991), Indian Circus (Chronicle, 1993 and Takarajimasha Inc., 1993), Portraits (Motta Fotografica, 1995 and Smithsonian, 1997), A Cry for Help (Simon & Schuster, 1996), Mary Ellen Mark: American Odyssey (Aperture, 1999), Mary Ellen Mark 55 (Phaidon, 2001), Photo Poche: Mary Ellen Mark (Nathan, 2002), Twins (Aperture, 2003), Exposure (Phaidon, 2005), Extraordinary Child (The National Museum of Iceland 2007) and Seen Behind the Scene (Phaidon, 2009). Mark's photographs have been exhibited worldwide.

She also acted as the Associate Producer of the major motion picture, American Heart (1992), directed by Martin Bell.

Her book, Exposure, is a large retrospective book published by Phaidon Press. It showcases 134 of Mary Ellen's best images, including both iconic and previously unpublished images. Her recent book and exhibition project, Extraordinary Child, was commissioned by the National Museum of Iceland, and features photographs of children at two specialized schools for the disabled in Reykjavik. Martin Bell also made a film on the same subject, which premiered at the exhibition.

Aside from her book and magazine work, Mark has photographed advertising campaigns, among which are Barnes & Noble, British Levis, Coach Bags, Eileen Fisher, Hasselblad, Heineken, Keds, Mass Mutual, Nissan and Patek Philippe.

Kevin O'Callaghan

Kevin O'Callaghan is a design educator with a unique focus on transformative conceptualization. O'Callaghan has been teaching 3-D design courses at the School of Visual Arts since 1985. In 1999, he founded the undergraduate 3-D design program, which he currently chairs. In collaboration, he and his students transform wasteful, dangerous, obsolete and iconic objects, products and "other" things into conceptual products and works of art. He has become well-known for his dynamic touring exhibitions, notably "Yugo Next," where each of 30 students were given one of the infamously bad Yugo automobiles and told to repurpose it into another functional object. It didn't work as a car, so he challenged his students to give it a new use. From car into gigantic telephone, grand piano, and even a church confessional booth, his students were required to develop a narrative from which the end product results. The exhibit filled Vanderbilt Hall in New York City's Grand Central Terminal, and went on to travel the world for over 2.5 years. This was just one of over 70 thematic exhibits that went on to be seen in many of the world's greatest venues. The exhibitions have been featured in over 190 newscasts and 400 articles reaching over 500 markets around the world, including CNN seven times. All of this exposure has given tremendous attention to all students involved.

While many of his projects and commissions bring forth the whimsical, O'Callaghan also engages in social and political commentary. For the past 30 years, sustainability has been a key component of many of O'Callaghan's creations. In 2008, NBC's Green is Universal commissioned O'Callaghan to create a piece of art to be on display in Rockefeller Plaza in celebration of "Earth Week." The art was shown on *The Today Show* every day that week, and viewed by over 40 million people across the country. The result was a 16 x 24 foot gold ornate frame constructed from all "Green" materials. Then, collaborating with his students, he created a piece of art made up of 5,000 cell phones (e-waste). Every day, a new panel was hung as *The Today Show* followed the progress of the cell phone art. At the end of the week the artwork was completed. The 2009 "Off-Roading" project took a fuel-indulgent truck off the highway and

gave it new life by converting its parts into household furnishings, including working lamps, chairs, tables, a couch and a chaise lounge. O'Callaghan mounted the "Disarm" exhibitio n in 2006, which repurposed M16 assault rifles into icons of a nonviolent society: the sanctity of a white picket fence, the sounds of a violin and the security of a teddy bear.

As an educator, O'Callaghan possesses a rare combination of indomitable fortitude and immeasurable tenderness. He is a demanding teacher who gives his students all that he can, and expects them to work at leastas hard as he does in helping them to achieve their visions. He instills in his students both the strength and confidence that "they can accomplish anything" with creativity and hard work. The wisdom of everything in moderation eludes O'Callaghan; his is a realm based upon the paradoxical, encompassing Foucault's "thinking the unthinkable" and Voltaire's reasoning that "the superfluous is a very necessary thing." He's been known to have a quick fuse under pressure and to react with verve, often accompanied by audible projection and a face as red as his hair.

As a 3-D designer, O'Callaghan also creates monumental imaginative spectaculars for clients including MTV, History Channel, NBC and other media giants. O'Callaghan is the designer of the iconic "Popcorn" Trophy for the MTV Movie Awards. O'Callaghan has become known as the guy who can make huge objects and deliver them overnight. His ability to produce at warp speed is unparalleled. But he takes the most pride in the work he does as a designer/ educator. His long-term relationship with the School of Visual Arts has produced many outcomes. His ART IS...HEALING poster, a tribute to the heroes of 9/11 has been included in the Library of Congress. He was the recipient of the ADC Gold Cube Award, Distinguished Artist– Teacher Award and a multiple- time recipient of the Platinum Teacher, Graphis New Talent

Annual award. In 2010, Harry N. Abrams published *Monumental*, a profusely illustrated chronicle of his many accomplishments.

Part cultural anthropologist and part creative whiz kid, O'Callaghan possesses a mature artistic vision that coexists with that cusp of life where the tooth fairy is alive and well, seductively inviting the fanciful to flourish. Yet for all the razzmatazz and grandeur that contributes to his creative ingenuity, when he shares an exploit, he becomes fully submerged in the moment, as though reliving the experience— the smells, colors, sights and sounds. Ultimately, O'Callaghan's symphonies are composed of textured dialogues through which disparate elements are repurposed and interwoven: a moon man makes orange juice and an old Olivetti typewriter becomes a birdcage.

Deborah Sussman

Deborah Sussman pioneered the field called "Environmental Graphic Design." Her contributions to "urban branding" have been internationally applauded, and influenced generations of designers.

Her education and training began with scholarships to Bard College and the Institute of Design (ID) in Chicago. At 22, she was invited to join the office of Charles and Ray Eames. During her 10-year affiliation, she played a significant role developing graphics, toys, exhibits, showrooms and films.

She has studied and worked in France, Germany (on a Fulbright Grant), Italy, Mexico and India, always photographing street life and indigenous cultures.

Early on, as a member of Los Angeles' growing art community, she designed a series of catalogs for the Los Angeles County Museum of Art. One, along with a video interview of her, is featured in the ongoing LACMA exhibit "California Design" (part of the huge "Pacific Standard Time" program).

Having established her own office in 1968 (later incorporated as Sussman/ Prejza in 1980 after marrying Paul Prejza), she continues to practice today. Her work is populist, exuberant and informed with a special gift for color. S/P and Deborah have collaborated with some of the finest architects of our times, including Frank Gehry, Philip Johnson, Foster Partners, GGN, Olin, MRY, Barton Myers and SOM.

Deborah and S/P led the design team globally celebrated for the 1984 Olympics in Los Angeles, together with the Jerde Partnership. Considered a turning point in the history of the Olympic Games, the "look" of "L.A. 84" appeared twice in *TIME* Magazine, influencing all subsequent Olympics.

S/P has, and continues, to design venues in the cultural sector, including the New Jersey Performing Arts Center, Seattle's McCaw Hall and MoAD (Museum of the African Diaspora) in San Francisco.

S/P has also enjoyed long-term relationships with clients ranging from Hasbro, the Rouse Company, Disney Development, Maguire-Thomas Partners, to the cities of Santa Monica and Culver City, the Southern California Gas Company, Mori Building Company (Japan), AMGEN and SC Johnson.

Recent and ongoing projects include branding the new "Grand Park" in downtown L.A.; design concepts for the L.A. Metro system; the Hollywood W Hotel; campuses at UC Berkeley and UCLA; and a global interior branding system for a long-term international client as well as several U.S. embassies.

Deborah spearheaded the much-applauded recent "Eames Words" exhibit at the A+D Museum in L.A. Her curatorial and design leadership provided insight into the daily lives of Charles and Ray. Instead of looking "as though the Eameses had designed it," this show revealed their delight in "the uncommon beauty of common things," but in a truly contemporary setting.

SELECT HONORS INCLUDE:

Golden Arrow Award (SEGD), 2006

Medalist, American Institute of
Graphic Arts (AIGA), 2004

Fellow, AIG /LA (2002)

Doctor of Humane Letters
(Bard College), 1998

First woman to exhibit in New
York's School of Visual Arts'
"Master Series," 1995

Fellow, Society of Environmental
Graphic Design (SEGD), 1991

Honorary Member, American
Institute of Architects (AIA), 1988

Alliance Graphique Internationale
(AGI), Elected Member, 1987

Founder, AIGA/LA, 1983

Her work has been featured in
Abitare, *Architectural Record*,
Architecture, *Design Quarterly*,
Domus, *Graphis*, *Grid*, *Metropolis*,
and *Print*, *Progressive Architecture*,
Process Architecture (Japan) as
well as the *Los Angeles Times*,
The New York Times,
The New Yorker, *TIME* Magazine
and numerous books.

Cumulative

Cumulative
Awards

Audience
Award

COMPANY: Mirada and SYPartners
ENTRY TITLE: THINK: An Exploration
Into Making the World Work Better
CLIENT: IBM

Design Team
of the Year

The New York Times Magazine

Advertising
Agency
of the Year

BETC

Network
of the Year

BBDO

School
of the Year

School of Visual Arts

Creating social change has always been tough.

ArtDirectorsClub

De
sign
ism

This category celebrates work that has made a significant impact on society through a focus on social causes and political change.

This past holiday season, the Colombian military developed a strategic campaign to entice guerrilla fighters to lay down their arms. The military constructed several Christmas trees along a tactical guerrilla route through the jungle, in the hope that the non-violent gesture and display of holiday spirit would entice the fighters to demobilize and return home. When guerrillas approached the trees, movement sensors made them light up and display a banner announced the following message: "If Christmas can come to the jungle, you can come home. Everything is possible at Christmas." The campaign was broadcast and showcased on international media channels, major news websites, blogs and various social media outlets. Over 300 guerrillas have demobilized as a direct result of this campaign effort, a 30 percent increase from the previous year.

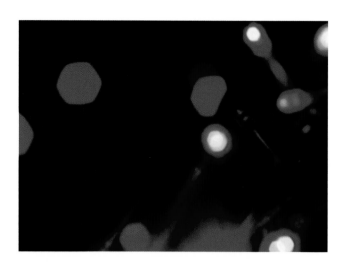

DAY 1
PLANNING:

OPERATION CHRISTMAS
LOWE/SSP3
ADVERTISING | Ambient/Environmental
Stunts/Guerrilla

CHAIRMAN: Jose Miguel Sokoloff
EXECUTIVE CREATIVE DIRECTOR:
Alejandro Benavides
CREATIVE DIRECTOR: Santiago Mesa
SENIOR ART DIRECTOR:
Carlos Andres Rodriguez
COPYWRITER: Sergio Leon
DESIGNER: Alejandro Ussa
DIRECTOR: Jaime Gonzalez, Jose Maria Angel
PRODUCER: Jose Vicente Altamar
CLIENT: Ministry of Defense
COUNTRY: Colombia

2000 LED
CHRISTMAS LIGHTS

We hope that bringing this Christmas message to the guerrilla,

"Back to the Start" is a charming and engaging two-minute, stop-motion animated film commissioned by Chipotle as a branding campaign to emphasize the importance of a sustainable food system. Created jointly by CAA Marketing and Chipotle, it depicts the life of a farmer as he transforms his family farm into an industrial animal factory before seeing the errors of his ways and opting for a more sustainable future. Directed by filmmaker Johnny Kelly, the film's soundtrack is the song "The Scientist," a Coldplay classic sung by country music legend Willie Nelson. The film ran in 5,700 theaters nationwide, aired once on broadcast TV during the 2012 Grammy Awards, and has appeared as online banners, as well as on both Chipotle's dedicated website and on Facebook.com/chipotle.

CHIPOTLE'S BACK TO THE START
CREATIVE ARTISTS AGENCY
AND CHIPOTLE
ADVERTISING | Broadcast Craft | Animation

DIRECTOR: Johnny Kelly
PRODUCER: Liz Chan
PRODUCTION COMPANY: Nexus Productions
MUSIC SUPERVISION: David Leinheardt
(Duotone Audio Group)
MUSIC PRODUCER: Justin Stanley,
Doyle Bramhall
SONG: Willie Nelson covering Coldplay's
"The Scientist"
CONTENT MANAGER: Liz Graves
CLIENT: Chipotle
COUNTRY: United States

Design
is tougher
than ever.

Keep fighting the good fight.   ArtDirectorsClub

De. sign.

Anger, yelling, screaming, a bit of shoving, throwing of sharp objects, strong opinions, and that was all before I left the house the morning of the ADC judging. When I got to the 'Club' I witnessed miles, upon miles, upon miles of design entries, and just when I thought it was over, the very studious volunteers lifted up yet another layer of work for the judges' approval. All done with amazing efficiency and symmetry. The payoff? Some really great work, in every category from books to motion graphics. There were some real standouts but my hat goes off to the student entries. The level of thought and presentation quality was impressive and I remember thinking how happy I was to not have to compete with them for a job. I look forward to witnessing what the next generation of young talent brings to the rapidly changing world of graphic design.

Arem Duplessis
Design Jury Chair

Design Jury

Arem Duplessis
The New York Times Magazine
United States

Jakob Daschek
Syrup
United States

Eric Pike
Martha Stewart
United States

Roanne Adams
RoAndCo
United States

Alexey Fadeyev
Depot WPD
Russia

Neil Powell
The Office of Neil Powell
United States

Sam Baron
Fabrica S.p.A.
Italy

Leo Jung
WIRED
United States

Joe Shouldice
yesyesyes design
United States

Irma Boom
Graphic Designer
Netherlands

Bobby C. Martin Jr.
OCD | Original
Champions of Design
United States

Bonnie Siegler
Eight and a Half
United States

Monica Brand
Mogollon, Inc.
United States

Oliver Munday
Sole Proprietor at OMG
United States

Alexander Trochut
Whatever, Whenever
Spain

Rama Chorpash
Rama Chorpash Design
United States

Valeria Pesqueira
PESQUEIRA
Argentina

Matt Willey
Matt Willey
United Kingdom

The New York Times Magazine
May 8, 2011

WHAT HAPPENED TO AIR FRANCE FLIGHT 447? By Wil S. Hylton

**WHAT HAPPENED TO AIR FRANCE
FLIGHT 447?**
THE NEW YORK TIMES MAGAZINE
Magazine Editorial | Cover

DESIGN DIRECTOR: Arem Duplessis
ART DIRECTOR: Gail Bichler
DEPUTY ART DIRECTOR: Caleb Bennett
DESIGNER: Caleb Bennett, Arem Duplessis
DIRECTOR OF PHOTOGRAPHY: Kathy Ryan

PHOTO EDITOR: Stacey Baker
PHOTOGRAPHER: Tom Sandberg
PUBLISHER: The New York Times Magazine
CLIENT: The New York Times Magazine
COUNTRY: United States

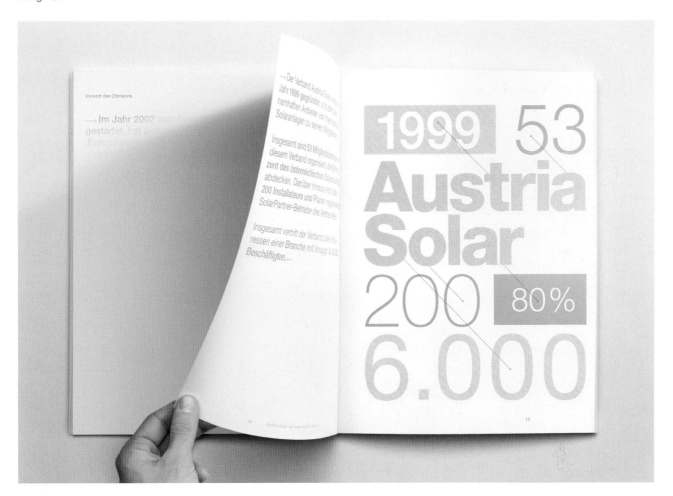

THE SOLAR ANNUAL REPORT
SERVICEPLAN GRUPPE FUR
INNOVATIVE KOMMUNIKATION
GMBH & CO. KG
Corporate/Promotional Design | Annual Report

CHIEF CREATIVE OFFICER: Alex Schill
CREATIVE DIRECTOR: Christoph Everke,
Cosimo Möller, Alexander Nagel
ART DIRECTOR: Matthäus Frost
COPYWRITER: Moritz Dornig
DESIGNER: Mathias Nösel
PRODUCTION COMPANY: mory & meier GmbH,
Buchbinderei Ruffert
ACCOUNT DIRECTOR: Christina Paulus,
Stefanie Zillner
CLIENT: Austria Solar
COUNTRY: Germany

DESIGN | Book Design | Typography

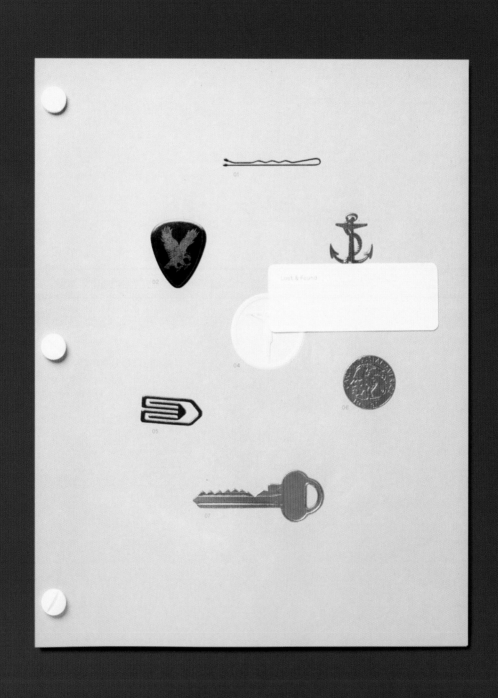

LOST & FOUND
HAPPY F&B
Corporate/Promotional Design
Booklet/Brochure

ART DIRECTOR: Oskar Andersson,
Gaioo Phunwut
ILLUSTRATOR: Moa Pårup
PROJECT MANAGER: Cecilia Holmström
CLIENT: Göteborgstryckeriet
COUNTRY: Sweden

02

06

HANDMADE CALENDAR FOR 2011
AYRCREATIVE
Corporate/Promotional Design
Calendar or Appointment Book

CREATIVE DIRECTOR: Yuichi Muto
DESIGN DIRECTOR: Yumiko Yasuda
ART DIRECTOR: Yumiko Yasuda
COPYWRITER: Yuichi Muto
DESIGNER: Tomohiro Okazaki,
Maya Matsumoto, Mai Watanabe

ILLUSTRATOR: Tomohiro Okazaki, Maya
Matsumoto, Tomoko Ogura, Mariko Yamaguchi
PRODUCER: Tatsuru Yagi
CLIENT: Daichi-no-Mi
COUNTRY: Japan

ANAMORPHIC MIRROR
ART+COM IN COOPERATION
WITH COORDINATION
Environmental Design
Retail/Restaurant/Office/Outdoor or Vehicle

EXECUTIVE CREATIVE DIRECTOR:
Joachim Sauter
CREATIVE DIRECTOR: Joachim Sauter
SENIOR ART DIRECTOR: Eva Offenberg
DESIGNER: Simon Häcker
PROJECT MANAGER: Gert Monath
CLIENT: Deutsche Bank AG
COUNTRY: Germany

MT TRAIN, MT EXPO,
MT EX HIROSHIMA
IYAMA DESIGN INC.
Environmental Design
Retail/Restaurant/Office/Outdoor or Vehicle

CREATIVE DIRECTOR: Koji Iyama
ART DIRECTOR: Koji Iyama
DESIGNER: Mayuko Watanabe,
Takenori Sugimura
PRODUCTION COMPANY: Iyama Design Inc.
PROJECT MANAGER: Yukio Taniguchi
ACCOUNT DIRECTOR: Shin Takatsuka
CLIENT: Kamoi Kakoshi Co., Ltd.
COUNTRY: Japan

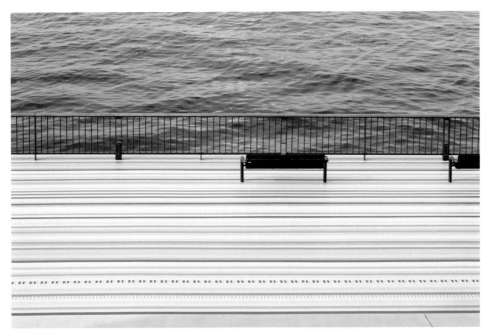

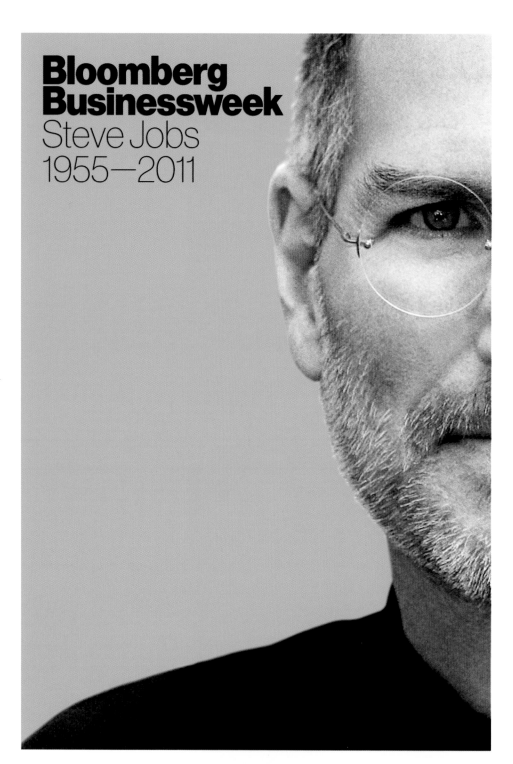

Bloomberg Businessweek
Steve Jobs
1955—2011

STEVE JOBS 1955–2011
BLOOMBERG BUSINESSWEEK
Magazine Editorial | Full Issue

CREATIVE DIRECTOR: Richard Turley
DESIGN DIRECTOR: Cynthia Hoffman
ART DIRECTOR: Robert Vargas, Jennifer Daniel
DESIGNER: Evan Applegate, Shawn Hasto,
Chandra Illick, Maayan Pearl,
Kenton Powell, Lee Wilson
DIRECTOR OF PHOTOGRAPHY: David Carthas
PHOTO EDITOR: Donna Cohen,
Jamie Goldenberg, Emily Keegin,
Diana Suryakusuma
PROJECT MANAGER: Emily Anton
COUNTRY: United States

And one more thing...

Remembering that you
are going to die
is the best way I know
to avoid the trap
of thinking you have
something to lose.

You are already naked.

There is no reason
not to follow your heart.

MALCOLM GLADWELL COLLECTED
BRIAN REA
Book Design | Limited Edition,
Private Press or Special Format Book

ART DIRECTOR: Paul Sahre
DESIGNER: Paul Sahre
ILLUSTRATOR: Brian Rea
PRODUCER: Josh Lieberson
CLIENT: Little, Brown and Company
COUNTRY: United States

**TWENTY-SIX CHARACTERS,
AN ALPHABETICAL JOURNEY
AROUND NOKIA'S NEW
TYPEFACE, NOKIA PURE.**

NOKIA DESIGN/
VISUAL COMMUNICATIONS
Book Design | Typography

DESIGN DIRECTOR: Iván Mato, Lisbet Tonner
ART DIRECTOR: Hugh Miller, Bradley Zimber
COPY EDITOR: Lisa Desforges
DESIGNER: George Chevalier Lewis,
Samuel Clarke, Steve Foyle, Troy Hyde,
Brody Larson, Tyrone Lou,
Gisele Palatnik, Nuno Silva
EDITOR: Aapo Bovellan, Chris Merrick
PUBLISHER: Gestalten
PROJECT MANAGER: Tiina Ruohonen,
Elisabeth Honerla
CLIENT: Nokia
COUNTRY: United Kingdom

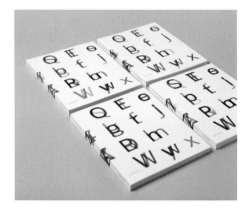

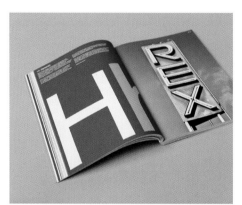

BE NOISY
HAKUHODO INC.
Poster Design | Promotional

CREATIVE DIRECTOR: Rikako Nagashima
ART DIRECTOR: Rikako Nagashima
DESIGNER: Rikako Nagashima, Naonori Yago
PHOTOGRAPHER: Yasutomo Ebisu
PRODUCER: Kazuhiro Hoshimoto
HAIR/MAKEUP: Katsuya Kamo
CLIENT: Laforet Harajuku
COUNTRY: Japan

be noisy. LAFORET

be noisy. **LAFORET**

Apple Store, Grand Central. XX.XX.XXXX
New Yorkers can do more in 60 seconds than anyone else.
And the busiest spot in The City is often Grand Central.
So we've got to make every second count. By having drop-in
Genius Bar appointments. By innovating new ways to get
customers in and out quickly. And by giving each customer
our undivided attention. Let's help our customers do more
than they ever thought possible, even if they only have a
second to spare.

**GRAND CENTRAL STATION APPLE
STORE OPENING**
APPLE MARKETING COMMUNICATIONS
Poster Design | Promotional

CLIENT: Apple
COUNTRY: United States

Foil Stamping Machine
Gletz AG
U www.gletz.com
T +41 71 388 22 22
F +41 71 388 22 23

Works of
**International
Graphic
Arts
Show**

Engraving
hinderer+mühlich KG
U www.hinderer-muehlich.de
T +49 7161 9 78 22–0
F +49 7161 9 78 22–10

Sep. 16 — 21, 2011

Direction
Iwai Tsusho K.K.
U www.iwai-tsusho.com
T 03 5810 6361
F 03 5810 6363

Paper
—
Sappi Fine Paper Europe
www.sappi.com

Foil
—
Kurz Japan Ltd.
www.kurzjapan.com

Processing
—
Bihaku Watanabe Company
www.bihaku-w.co.jp

Graphic Design
—
AD&D
www.ad-and-d.jp

Copyright © 2011 Iwai Tsusho K.K.and AD&D All Rights Reserved

**WORKS OF INTERNATIONAL
GRAPHIC ARTS SHOW**
AD&D
Poster Design | Typography

ART DIRECTOR: Ren Takaya
DESIGNER: Ren Takaya
DIRECTOR: Mitsuru Sato
EXECUTIVE PRODUCER: Katsuhiro Kagota
PRODUCTION COMPANY:
Bihaku Watanabe Company
TYPOGRAPHER: Ren Takaya
PROJECT MANAGER: Hideyuki Watanabe
CLIENT: IWAI TSUSHO K.K.
COUNTRY: Japan

Date 比賽日期

Tung Chung
Man Tung Road Sports Centre
東涌文東路體育館

Venue 比賽地點

G/F., Tung Chung Municipal Services Building,
39 Man Tung Road, Tung Chung
東涌文東路39號，東涌市政大樓地下

THE 19TH
ITF TAEKWONDO
CHAMPIONSHIP
第十九届ITF跆拳道大赛

Organisation 主辦團體

designed by www.cpluscworkshop.com

JOHN & JOHN
PETER SCHMIDT GROUP
Package Design | Food / Beverage

CLIENT: Market Grounds GmbH & Co. KG
COUNTRY: Germany

DESIGN NORI

wish for peace of sea and human.
created in 2011
by Umino seaweed shop.

1. THE BRIEF

Our client is a traditional nori (seaweed) manufacturer in north East Japan. Having struggled with a long declining sales trend, and with damage from the massive tsunami that swept away their factories, the client asked us to design new packaging that could boost their products' appeal to a modern urban audience.

2. THE CHALLENGES

How can we make a black square of seaweed interesting?
The basic shape design of a square of nori – mostly used for sushi rolls – has not changed since its creation in the early 15th century. Nori itself is an ordinary square that it might be the last product that people would think of as modern, regardless of the packaging.

3. The Reason Why We Created that Design

Rather than focus exclusively on packaging, we applied design to the product itself. We wanted to make nori the focus – to have it talked about by an urban, design-conscious target audience.
We used laser cutters to carve designs into our nori – classic patterns from Japanese history called MonYo that signify growth, beauty, long life, etc. Themes we thought that could uplift people following the tsunami. The nori remains functional, but by combining tradition with modern technology, we created an entirely new type of nori never seen before – one that conveys our hopes for the future, as well as our respect for the past.

桜 SAKURA 水玉 MIZUTAMA 麻の葉 ASANOHA 亀甲 KIKKO 組亀甲 KUMIKIKKO

DESIGN NORI (SEAWEED)
I&S BBDO INC.
Product Design | Gift/Specialty Product

EXECUTIVE CREATIVE DIRECTOR:
Yoshihisa Ogata
CREATIVE DIRECTOR: Kenichiro Shigetomi
ART DIRECTOR: Kenichiro Shigetomi
COPYWRITER: Kiyoyuki Enomoto
DESIGNER: Kenichiro Shigetomi
DIRECTOR: Ririko Murata
PRODUCER: Koji Onishi
CLIENT: Umino Seaweed Store
COUNTRY: Japan

BRONZE: DESIGN
Product Design | Food/Beverage

THE STEVE JOBS MOMENT OF SILENCE
KNARF®
Product Design | Miscellaneous

EXECUTIVE CREATIVE DIRECTOR:
Frank Anselmo
ART DIRECTOR: Hyui Yong Kim,
Bryan Wolff Schoemaker
COPYWRITER: Bryan Wolff Schoemaker,
Hyui Yong Kim
DESIGNER: Bryan Wolff Schoemaker,
Hyui Yong Kim
PROGRAMMER: Yong Wolff
CLIENT: Moment of Silence Inc.
COUNTRY: United States

The Steve Jobs Moment of Silence

**The 8 seconds of silence in your iTunes library
symbolize the 8 years Steve Jobs fought pancreatic cancer.
Proceeds are donated to several pancreatic cancer organizations:**
*The Pancreatic Cancer Action Network®, The Lustgarten Foundation®
and The Hirshberg Foundation for Pancreatic Cancer Research®*

$0.99 Buy

Released: Dec 19, 2011
Ⓟ 2011 Moment of Silence Inc.

**This small break in our iTunes library will remind us
to never forget the man who brought us:**

COLORS ISSUE NO. 81 -
TRANSPORT: A SURVIVAL GUIDE
FABRICA S.P.A.
Magazine Editorial | Full Issue

CREATIVE DIRECTOR: Patrick Waterhouse
ART DIRECTOR: Grégory Ambos,
Henriette Kruse Jørgenses
COPYWRITER: Cosimo Bizzarri,
Jonah Goodman, Juan Pablo Gallón Salazar
COPY EDITOR: Tom Ridgway
DESIGNER: Florian Jakober
ILLUSTRATOR: James Graham,
Namyoung An, Patrick Waterhouse
DIRECTOR OF PHOTOGRAPHY:
James Mollison
PHOTOGRAPHER: James Mollison,
Alfredo D'amato, Rajesh Vora,
David Høgsholt, Boris Austin
ANIMATOR: Martin Engh
DIRECTOR: Enrico Bossan
EDITOR: Jonah Goodman
HEAD OF PRODUCTION: Mauro Bedoni
PHOTO EDITOR: Mauro Bedoni
RETOUCHER: Diego Beyró
PUBLISHER: Fabrica
CLIENT: COLORS MAGAZINE - FABRICA
COUNTRY: Italy

VOL.33 AUTUMN/WINTER 2011/12
KID'S WEAR VERLAG
Magazine Editorial | Full Issue

ART DIRECTOR: Mike Meiré
PHOTO EDITOR: Ann-Katrin Weiner
PUBLISHER: Achim Lippoth
CLIENT: kid's wear Magazine
COUNTRY: Germany

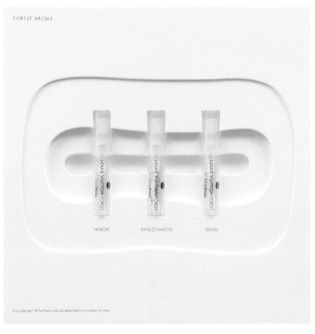

LOUIS VUITTON FOREST BOX
Book Design | Limited Edition, Private Press
or Special Format Book

ART DIRECTOR: Hiroaki Nagai
DESIGNER: Hiroaki Nagai, Daisuke Yajima
PHOTOGRAPHER: Mikiya Takimoto
CLIENT: Louis Vuitton Japan
COUNTRY: Japan

SIMON BEATTIE IDENTITY
PURPOSE
Corporate/Promotional Design
Booklet/Brochure

CREATIVE DIRECTOR: Rob Howsam
DESIGNER: Paul Felton, Amie Herriott
RETOUCHER: Matt Welch
PROJECT MANAGER: Lynsey Mackay
CLIENT: Simon Beattie
COUNTRY: United Kingdom

CIRCULAR 17
PENTAGRAM DESIGN
Magazine Editorial | Full Issue

CHAIRMAN: John Bateson
DESIGN DIRECTOR: Domenic Lippa
COPY EDITOR: Val Kildea, Louise Sloper
DESIGNER: Domenic Lippa, Jeremy Kunze
TYPOGRAPHER: Jeremy Kunze
CLIENT: The Typographic Circle
COUNTRY: United Kingdom

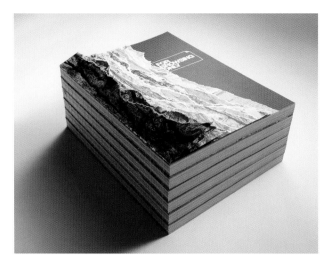

FOR BROWSING ONLY
A BEAUTIFUL DESIGN
Book Design | Limited Edition, Private Press
or Special Format Book

CREATIVE DIRECTOR: Roy Poh
COPYWRITER: Roy Poh
DESIGNER: Roy Poh
PHOTOGRAPHER: John Nursalim
PUBLISHER: A Beautiful Design
CLIENT: The Browsing Copy Project
COUNTRY: Singapore

**"WORLD SUMMIT AND CONGRESS
OF ARCHITECTURE, DESIGN AND
PLANNING MONTREAL 2017"
BROCHURE**

PAPRIKA
Corporate/Promotional Design
Booklet/Brochure

CREATIVE DIRECTOR: Louis Gagnon
ART DIRECTOR: Daniel Robitaille
CLIENT: Mission Design
COUNTRY: Canada

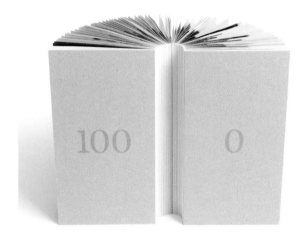

0 TO 100 BOOK
UP INC
Book Design | Limited Edition, Private Press
or Special Format Book

CREATIVE DIRECTOR: Carey George
ART DIRECTOR: Ryan Booth
COPYWRITER: Lisa Devries
COPY EDITOR: Sue McCluskey
DESIGNER: Ryan Booth
PHOTOGRAPHER: Sandy Nicholson
RETOUCHER: The Gas Company
PROJECT MANAGER:
Barbara Wodnicka-Anderson
CLIENT: Up Inc
COUNTRY: Canada

**MR. LEE, TAILOR TO SUPERHEROS
AND VILLAINS**
LEO BURNETT IBERIA
Corporate/Promotional Design | Miscellaneous

CHAIRMAN: Isabel Ontoso
EXECUTIVE CREATIVE DIRECTOR:
Chacho Puebla
CREATIVE DIRECTOR: Juan Sevilla,
Juan Christmann
SENIOR ART DIRECTOR: Juan Sevilla
ART DIRECTOR: Bruno Nakano
COPYWRITER: Juan Christmann
DESIGNER: Bruno Nakano
PHOTOGRAPHER: David Vega Corrochano
PROGRAMMER: Victor Moreno
ACCOUNT DIRECTOR: Asier García
CLIENT: Sony Playstation DC Universe Online
COUNTRY: Spain

GRAPHIC EXPLANATION
TOKYU AGENCY INC.
Poster Design | Typography

CREATIVE DIRECTOR: Tatsuki Ikezawa
DESIGN DIRECTOR: Tatsuki Ikezawa
ART DIRECTOR: Tatsuki Ikezawa
COPYWRITER: Hiroyuki Nishio
DESIGNER: Takemichi Chiba, Hiromi Fukui
ILLUSTRATOR: Takemichi Chiba, Hiromi Fukui

TYPOGRAPHER: Tatsuki Ikezawa
PUBLISHER: Maki Yoshimura
PROJECT MANAGER: Maki Yoshimura
CLIENT: PIE International
COUNTRY: Japan

SHIBAURA HOUSE
SMBETSMB
Corporate/Promotional Design | Logo/Trademark

ART DIRECTOR: Keita Shimbo, Misaco Shimbo
DESIGNER: Keita Shimbo, Misaco Shimbo
CLIENT: Kohihoku Seihan Inc.
COUNTRY: Japan

SEAT TYPOGRAPHY
LUKAS LINDEMANN ROSINSKI GMBH
Poster Design | Typography

EXECUTIVE CREATIVE DIRECTOR:
Arno Lindemann, Bernhard Lukas
CREATIVE DIRECTOR: Thomas Heyen,
Markus Kremer
ART DIRECTOR: Soen Becker

COPYWRITER: Tim Esser, Jan Hoffmeister
PROGRAMMER: David Soukup
ACCOUNT DIRECTOR: Jascha Oevermann
CLIENT: Mercedes-Benz Vans
COUNTRY: Germany

BLACK&BLUE PACKAGE
HAKUHODO INC.
Package Design | Fashion/Apparel/Wearable

CREATIVE DIRECTOR: Masato Fukuhara
ART DIRECTOR: Ryota Sakae
DESIGNER: Yuhei Ito, Yasuyuki Okamoto
CLIENT: White Lodge Co., Ltd.
COUNTRY: Japan

Magic

1day Menicon Flat Pack

MAGIC - CONCEPT BOOK
(DISPOSABLE CONTACT LENS)
DENTSU+DRILL+PARTY
Corporate/Promotional Design |
Booklet/Brochure

CREATIVE DIRECTOR: Morihiro Harano
ART DIRECTOR: Yoshihiro Yagi
COPYWRITER: Haruko Tsutsui
DESIGNER: Toshimitsu Tanaka, Ayano Higa
PHOTOGRAPHER: Takaya Sakano
EXECUTIVE PRODUCER: Koji Wada
PRODUCER: Tetsuji Nose
LINE PRODUCER: Takeshi Arimoto
PRODUCTION COMPANY: Katachi Co., Ltd.
RETOUCHER: Yosuke Mochizuki
ACCOUNT DIRECTOR: Dai Sakashita
CLIENT: Menicon Co., Ltd.
COUNTRY: Japan

Magic Disposable Contact Lens for
DESIGN | Package Design | Miscellaneous

STINA
BRANDOCTOR & BRUKETA&ŽINIĆ OM
Package Design | Food/Beverage

SENIOR BRAND CONSULTANT:
Anja Bauer Minkara
BRAND CONSULTANT: Petra Depot
CREATIVE DIRECTOR: Davor Bruketa,
Nikola Zinic
ART DIRECTOR: Davor Bruketa, Nikola Zinic
COPYWRITER: Anja Bauer Minkara,
Maja Bencic
DESIGNER: Sonja Surbatovic
HEAD OF PRODUCTION: Vesna Durasin
PROJECT MANAGER: Jelena Mezga
CLIENT: Jako vino
COUNTRY: Croatia

CREATIVE DIRECTOR: Morihiro Harano

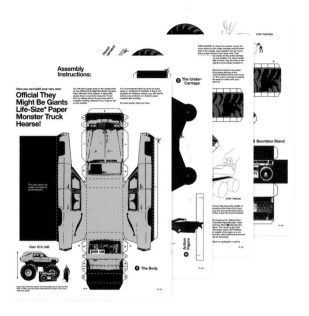

JOIN US
OFFICE OF PAUL SAHRE
Package Design | Entertainment

CREATIVE DIRECTOR: John Flansburgh
ART DIRECTOR: Paul Sahre
DESIGNER: Paul Sahre, Elias Derboven,
Erik Carter, Santiago Carrasquilla,
Alex Stikeleather

ILLUSTRATOR: Paul Sahre, Erik Carter
PHOTOGRAPHER: Joe Hollier
DIRECTOR: Paul Sahre, Joe Hollier
EDITOR: Tony Zajkowski, Joe Hollier
PRODUCER: John Flansburgh, Paul Sahre
MUSIC/COMPOSER: They Might be Giants
CLIENT: They Might Be Giants
COUNTRY: United States

CASS ART OWN BRAND
PENTAGRAM DESIGN
Package Design | Gift/Specialty Product

DESIGN DIRECTOR: Angus Hyland
DESIGNER: Angus Hyland,
Fabian Hermann, Alex Johns
ILLUSTRATOR: Angus Hyland,
Fabian Hermann, Alex Johns

CLIENT: Cass Art
COUNTRY: United Kingdom

SMITH. FOOD FOR THE EVERYMAN.
LEO BURNETT TORONTO
Environmental Design |
Retail/Restaurant/Office/Outdoor or Vehicle

CHIEF CREATIVE OFFICER: Judy John
CREATIVE DIRECTOR: Lisa Greenberg
DESIGNER: Scott Leder,
Chris Duchaine, Tracy Ma

INTERIOR DESIGNER: Commute Home
PHOTOGRAPHER: David Picard
CLIENT: Smith Restaurant + Bar
COUNTRY: Canada

D&AD GRADUATE ACADEMY
THE CHASE CREATIVE CONSULTANTS
Branding | Campaign

CREATIVE DIRECTOR: Oliver Maltby,
Ben Casey
DESIGN DIRECTOR: Chris Challinor
ART DIRECTOR: Rebecca Low
DESIGNER: Rebecca Low, Dulcie Cowling

PHOTOGRAPHER: Paul Thompson
CLIENT: D&AD and Hewlett-Packard
COUNTRY: United Kingdom

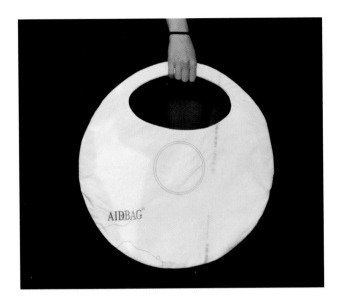

AIDBAG
JUNG VON MATT AG
Product Design | Fashion/Apparel/Wearable

EXECUTIVE CREATIVE DIRECTOR:
Mathias Stiller, Armin Jochum
CREATIVE DIRECTOR: Christian Kroll,
Peter Gocht
ART DIRECTOR: Javier Suarez Argueta
COPYWRITER: Bjoern Ingenleuf
EDITOR: Sascha Gerlach,
Perisade Mashayekhi

PRODUCER: Julia Cramer
PRODUCTION COMPANY:
Jung von Matt/Spree GmbH
PROJECT MANAGER: Marie Braun,
Stefanie Gombert
ART BUYER: Marjorie Jorrot
CLIENT: Daimler AG
COUNTRY: Germany

THE BRANDSPACE
ART+COM IN COOPERATION WITH
COORDINATION, BERLIN
Environmental Design |
Retail/Restaurant/Office/Outdoor or Vehicle

CHIEF CREATIVE OFFICER:
Joachim Sauter, Jochen Gringmuth
ART DIRECTOR: Eva Offenberg, Petra Trefzger
DESIGNER: Arne Michel, Christian Riekoff
PROGRAMMER: Sebastian Heymann,
Robert Chudoba

PROJECT MANAGER: Gert Monath
CLIENT: Deutsche Bank AG
COUNTRY: Germany

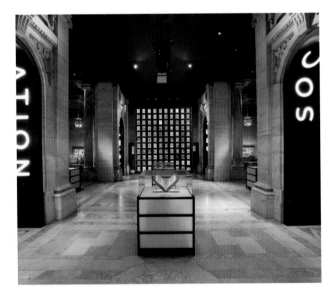

**NEW YORK PUBLIC LIBRARY,
CELEBRATING 100 YEARS
EXHIBITION**
PENTAGRAM DESIGN
Environmental Design |
Gallery/Museum Installation

DESIGN DIRECTOR: Michael Gericke
ART DIRECTOR: Michael Gericke
DESIGNER: Don Bilodeau, Jed Skillins,
Matt McInerney
PHOTOGRAPHER: Peter Mauss (Esto)

CURATOR: Thomas Mellins
PROJECT MANAGER: Gillian DeSousa
CLIENT: New York Public Library
COUNTRY: United States

OBSTFIGUREN (FRUIT FIGURES)
SCHOLZ & FRIENDS BERLIN GMBH
Product Design | Food/Beverage

EXECUTIVE CREATIVE DIRECTOR: Martin Pross
CHIEF CREATIVE OFFICER: Wolf Schneider,
Matthias Spaetgens
CREATIVE DIRECTOR: Mathias Rebmann,
Florian Schwalme
SENIOR ART DIRECTOR: Loic Sattler
ART DIRECTOR: Jinhi Kim, Björn Kernspeckt,
René Gebhardt
COPYWRITER: Alexander Döpel, Sandra Krebs
DESIGNER: Simon Rossow, Peter Schönherr
FOOD DESIGN: Volker Hobl

PHOTOGRAPHER: Attila Hartwig
ASSISTANT TO THE PHOTOGRAPHER:
Cosima Walther
PHOTO EDITOR: Maren Boerner
RETOUCHER: Maren Boerner
PROJECT MANAGER: Anna Kubitza,
Masa Matejic
ACCOUNT DIRECTOR: Benjamin Baader,
Sebastian Vetter, Miriam Spahrbier
CLIENT: Fresh 'N' Friends
COUNTRY: Germany

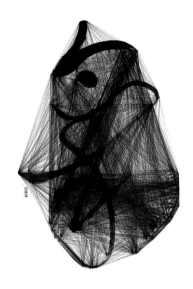

KENT 'VOL' PROJECT
OGILVY & MATHER JAPAN
Product Design
Electronics, Appliances, or Housewares

EXECUTIVE CREATIVE DIRECTOR:
David Morgan, Shingo Ichimura
CREATIVE DIRECTOR: Shoji Tamura
DESIGN DIRECTOR: Hironao Tsuboi
ART DIRECTOR: Takahisa Hashimoto
COPYWRITER: Takahisa Hashimoto

DESIGNER: Takanori Kimura, Kiyoshi Imafuji,
Eriko Wakabayashi
PROJECT MANAGER: Hiroaki Masuda
ACCOUNT DIRECTOR: Koichi Ishizu
CLIENT: British American Tabacco Japan
COUNTRY: Japan

**INGENUITY FOLLOWS
NATURE - SPIRITED**
HESIGN INTERNATIONAL GMBH
Poster Design | Typography

CREATIVE DIRECTOR: Jianping He
DESIGNER: Jianping He
PROGRAMMER: Dominique Schmitz
CLIENT: Asian Culture and Arts Development
COUNTRY: Germany

WE MAKE VOTING EASY
LEO BURNETT TORONTO
Branding | Campaign

CHIEF CREATIVE OFFICER: Judy John
CREATIVE DIRECTOR: Judy John,
Lisa Greenberg, Shirley Ward-Taggart
ART DIRECTOR: David Federico, Scott Leder,
Mike Morelli, Matthew Kenney, Ron Cueto,
Brendan Good
COPYWRITER: Morgan Kurchak, Josh Rachlis,
Len Preskow, Joy Panday
DESIGNER: Scott Leder, Chris Duchaine,
Kimberley Pereira, Jeff Watkins, Tracy Ma

ILLUSTRATOR: Chris Duchaine,
Kimberley Pereira, James Joyce
PHOTOGRAPHER: Jesse Senko
PRODUCER: Jacqueline Bellmore
PROJECT MANAGER: Cimmeron Kirk,
Kenneth Hor
ACCOUNT DIRECTOR: David Buckspan,
Danielle Iozzo, Tara Collins
CLIENT: Elections Ontario
COUNTRY: Canada

Design Merits

DOMENICA
IL SOLE 24 ORE
Newspaper Editorial | Insert

EDITOR IN CHIEF: Gianni Riotta
CREATIVE DIRECTOR: Luca Pitoni,
Adriano Attus
TYPOGRAPHER: Luciano Perondi (molotro)
PUBLISHER: Il Sole 24 Ore
CLIENT: Il Sole 24 Ore
COUNTRY: Italy

SIGNAGE SYSTEM AND INTERIOR
DESIGN: ADIDAS LACES 2011
BÜRO UEBELE VISUELLE
KOMMUNIKATION GMBH & CO. KG
Environmental Design |
Wayfinding Systems/Signage

DESIGN DIRECTOR: Andreas Uebele
DESIGNER: Carolin Himmel
PHOTOGRAPHER: Christian Richters,
Werner Huthmacher
PROJECT MANAGER: Carolin Himmel
CLIENT: adidas AG
COUNTRY: Germany

SWEET AND VICIOUS
THE NEW YORK TIMES MAGAZINE
Magazine Editorial | Cover

DESIGN DIRECTOR: Arem Duplessis
SENIOR ART DIRECTOR: Gail Bichler
ART DIRECTOR: Caleb Bennett
DESIGNER: Gail Bichler
DIRECTOR OF PHOTOGRAPHY: Kathy Ryan
PHOTOGRAPHER: Kenji Aoki
PHOTO EDITOR: Joanna Milter
PUBLISHER: The New York Times Magazine
CLIENT: The New York Times Magazine
COUNTRY: United States

TO/FROM 2.0
DESIGN ARMY
Product Design | Gift/Specialty Product

CREATIVE DIRECTOR: Pum Lefebure,
Jake Lefebure
ART DIRECTOR: Pum Lefebure
DESIGNER: Jackie Lay, Mariela Hsu
CLIENT: Design Army
COUNTRY: United States

CREATIVE WEEK NEW YORK IDENTITY
COLLINS
Corporate/Promotional Design |
Logo/Trademark

CHIEF CREATIVE OFFICER: Brian Collins
CREATIVE DIRECTOR: Leland Maschmeyer
DESIGNER: Matt Luckhurst
CLIENT: The One Club
COUNTRY: United States

THE HAND.WRITTEN.LETTER.PROJECT
MUSIC
Book Design | Limited Edition/Private
Press or Special Format Book

DESIGNER: Craig Oldham
ILLUSTRATOR: Marion Deuchars
PRODUCER: Shelley Wood
PUBLISHER: The Unified Theory Of Everything
CURATOR: Craig Oldham
PROJECT MANAGER: Shelley Wood
CLIENT: National Literacy Trust, KK Outlet
COUNTRY: United Kingdom

STRANGER & STRANGER
SPIRIT NO.13
STRANGER & STRANGER
Package Design |
Gift/Specialty Product

CREATIVE DIRECTOR: Kevin Shaw
DESIGNER: Guy Pratt, Cosimo Surace,
Ewa Oliver
ILLUSTRATOR: Thomas Bewick
CLIENT: Stranger & Stranger
COUNTRY: United States

BLACK&BLUE POSTER
HAKUHODO INC.
Poster Design | Promotional

CREATIVE DIRECTOR: Masato Fukuhara
ART DIRECTOR: Ryota Sakae
DESIGNER: Yuhei Ito, Yasuyuki Okamoto
PHOTOGRAPHER: Seiko Ishikawa
CLIENT: White Lodge Co., Ltd.
COUNTRY: Japan

SHE
BLOK DESIGN
Corporate/Promotional Design |
Stationery Series

CREATIVE DIRECTOR: Vanessa Eckstein,
Marta Cutler
COPYWRITER: Marta Cutler
DESIGNER: Vanessa Eckstein,
Patricia Kleeberg
CLIENT: SHE
COUNTRY: Canada

ARCHITECTURAL HARDWARE
COMPANY SMALL GRAPHICS
COSMOS
Corporate/Promotional Design |
Press/Promotional Kit

CREATIVE DIRECTOR: Yoshiki Uchida
ART DIRECTOR: Yoshiki Uchida
DESIGNER: Atushi Sugiyama
CLIENT: Koyama Kanamono
COUNTRY: Japan

TARGET HEAVY FOOD
BBDO PROXIMITY BERLIN GMBH
Package Design | Miscellaneous

CHIEF CREATIVE OFFICER: Jan Harbeck,
David Mously, Wolfgang Schneider
ART DIRECTOR: Daniel Schweinzer
COPYWRITER: Lukas Liske
ILLUSTRATOR: Daniel Schweinzer
HEAD OF PRODUCTION: Michael Pflanz
PRODUCTION COMPANY:
Pflanz Produktionsservice, Berlin
POST PRODUCTION:
Pirates 'N Paradise, Berlin
ACCOUNT MANAGER: Guelcan Demir
CLIENT: Medicom Pharma GmbH
COUNTRY: Germany

THE SPRINTER APPLIES FOR A JOB
LUKAS LINDEMANN ROSINSKI GMBH
Corporate/Promotional Design |
Miscellaneous

EXECUTIVE CREATIVE DIRECTOR:
Arno Lindemann, Bernhard Lukas
CREATIVE DIRECTOR: Thomas Heyen,
Markus Kremer, Jakob Kriwat

ART DIRECTOR:
Markus Kremer, Damian Kuczmierczyk
COPYWRITER: Thomas Heyen
DESIGNER: Victor Aloji
DIRECTOR: Marc Bethke
EXECUTIVE PRODUCER: Martin Schoen
PRODUCTION COMPANY:
Markenfilm Crossing
VISUAL EFFECTS: Thomas Beecken
PROJECT MANAGER: Jascha Oevermann
ACCOUNT DIRECTOR: Konstanze Kievenheim
CLIENT: Mercedes Benz Vans
COUNTRY: Germany

CHESTER ZOO RE-BRAND
MUSIC
Corporate Promotional Design |
Corporate Identity Program

CREATIVE DIRECTOR: Anthony Smith
ART DIRECTOR: Craig Oldham
COPYWRITER: Mike Reed
DESIGNER: Craig Oldham, Orla McGrath
ILLUSTRATOR: Adam Hayes
PROGRAMMER: Ian Mitchell
ACCOUNT DIRECTOR: Sue Strange
CLIENT: Chester Zoo
COUNTRY: United Kingdom

THE LAUNDRY-GALLERY
SCHOLZ & FRIENDS
Environmental Design |
Gallery/Museum Installation

EXECUTIVE CREATIVE DIRECTOR:
Matthias Spaetgens
CHIEF CREATIVE OFFICER: Martin Pross
CREATIVE DIRECTOR:
Robert Krause, Florian Schwalme,
Mathias Rebmann, Markus Daubenbuechel
ART DIRECTOR: Sebastian Kamp,
Bjoern Kernspeckt, Rene Gebhardt
COPYWRITER: Stefan Sohlau
GRAPHIC DESIGNER: Susan Wesarg,
Philipp Bertisch
PHOTOGRAPHER: Szymon Plewa
DIRECTOR: Til Obladen
PRODUCER: Nele Siegl, Daniel Klessig
ACCOUNT DIRECTOR: Kerstin Seidel,
Mehibe Tuncel
SCULPTURES: Szymon Plewa
CLIENT: Siemens Electrogeraete GmbH
COUNTRY: Germany

GROSSARTIG
BRANSCH INC.
Magazine Editorial | Full Issue

COPYWRITER: Kathy Ryan
DESIGNER: Christoph Steinegger (Interkool)
ILLUSTRATOR: Hara Katsiki
DIRECTOR OF PHOTOGRAPHY:
Susanne Bransch
PHOTOGRAPHER: Mauricio Alejo, AORTA,
Wim Bosch, Frieke Janssens, June-Louis,
Romain Laurent, Achim Lippoth, Joerg
Reichardt, Christian Stoll, Marina Weigl,
Ofer Wolberger, Kerstin zu Pa
EDITOR: Susanne Bransch
PUBLISHER: Abatenni Verlag
CLIENT: Grossartig Magazine
COUNTRY: United States

Photography is tougher than ever.

Keep fighting the good fight.

ArtDirectorsClub

Pho to to gra phy

This was a jury driven by gut. It's often hard to find the words to explain why a picture is successful, so once debate broke out, it often meant the demise of that image in the ranks. A great image is one that stops you, with its power, its seduction and sometimes the quiet curiosity it invokes. Beyond these primal reactions, all you are left to discuss is paper stock and retouching, along with details that ultimately trivialize what makes a standout photograph. Bluntly, the images that rose to the top were the best ones.

Kieran Antill
Photography Jury Chair

Photography Jury

Kieran Antill
Leo Burnett New York
United States

Simon Harsent
Photographer
United States

Nick Onken
Nick Onken Photography Inc.
United States

Kira Pollack
TIME Magazine
United States

Siung Tjia
Bloomberg Markets Magazine
United States

'9/11

STARTED OFF AS A REGULAR MORNING IN THE FIREHOUSE. WE
got a call around 8 o'clock for a gas leak in the street at Church
and Lispenard, about 12 blocks away from the World Trade
Center. It was a beautiful summer day, bright sunshine and
warm weather. While we were standing in the street, we
heard a loud roar of a plane. We saw it for a glance, and then
it was hidden behind some buildings. And when it appeared
again, I saw the plane aim and crash into the north tower of
the World Trade Center. I got on the radio and said, "A plane
just crashed into the World Trade Center." About a minute
later, after I was able to think a little bit and realize what was
taking place, I got back on the radio, and I said, "Battalion 1
to Manhattan: this looked like the plane was aiming for the
building. This was a direct attack."

We could see the smoke coming from the Trade Center. We
knew that at that moment, tens of thousands of people were in
the greatest need, and we had to do something. As the firefighters came in, the order was to go to the 70th floor. We figured
eight floors was a good margin of safety. I can remember one
lieutenant from Engine 33 came up to me and just looked. We
looked at each other, just concerned about whether we were
going to be O.K. I told that lieutenant to take his unit and go
up and start to evacuate and rescue those that were in trouble.
That was the last time I saw that lieutenant.

At 9:03 that morning, we heard another loud roar of a plane.
This time the plane crashed into the south tower. Now with two
towers on fire, we split our operations. The firefighters went in
and climbed to rescue those on the upper floors. But then, at
9:59, we heard this loud roar. I had really no idea what it was. We
thought maybe the elevators were blowing out or something
from the plane was crashing into the lobby. Then the entire
lobby went all black, and we heard this rumbling sound. I got on
the radio and said to all units in Tower 1, "Evacuate the building." But we made a slow retreat—because what you saw on TV
we did not see. We had no idea that an entire 110-story building
had just collapsed to the ground.

As we were ready to move from the lobby, I noticed there was
someone lying at my feet. It was Father Mychal Judge. I bent
down, I removed his white collar and checked for a pulse, and I
knew at that point that he was gone. See, Father Judge was with
us in the lobby, and usually when he's with us at fires, he would
have a smile and a glance—Hey, are you doing O.K.? But this

time was different. I saw in the lobby that he was praying—it
was like a physical prayer. I could see his lips move, and I could
see the stress on his face. It was no longer an ordinary fire.

Even standing in the street, we could not understand about
the collapse of the south tower. Then I remember hearing another
loud roar, and we started to run. This beautiful summer morning,
bright sunshine, went totally black. You couldn't see the hand in
front of your face. And then there was an eerie sound of silence.
All the chatter on the radio went quiet. You heard nothing. It was
like a new snowfall. It was just a muffled sound of silence.

That day, we continued to search for people, and we found
some, but not many. I remained at the Trade Center site till probably around 11 o'clock at night. The streets of New York were
totally dark. I walked into the firehouse. It was a very somber
mood. They told me that the people from Ladder 1, Engine 7—
the two companies that were in my firehouse—we all survived.
But we lost so many others. I remember being overly tired and
not being able to see because of the dust that went in my eyes. So
I drove back home. I knew my family would be worried. When
we met that evening around midnight, we embraced each other
with a lot of tears. The next morning, I got up around 6 and was
really unable to see. I called a friend, my college roommate,
who's a cardiologist, Tom Cunningham, and I said, "Tom, I can't
see too good. You've got to help me." He was able to give me an
eye doctor, who I met with every day for the next three weeks,
and he took 50 pieces, slivers of steel, out of my eyes.

That lieutenant I spoke about was my brother, and it was
good that we met. We recovered his remains in February 2002.
I rode in the back of the ambulance with him, which had to
be one of the saddest days of my life. But I can remember back
through tears and despair, starting to remember the good
things we did, like sailing—sailing on a beautiful summer day,
similar to the day of 9/11. Those memories and the memories of
so many other firefighters are the things that hold us together.

People ask, What does it mean to be a hero? I define heroes
as those who do ordinary things but in an extraordinary time.
That's what the firefighters did. They went up and did ordinary
things, like encouraging people to continue down, don't stop,
continue to walk. Climbing stairs with almost 100 pounds of
equipment, trying to get up to those who couldn't get out themselves. Ordinary things, but it was at this extraordinary time.

9/11 is not just a New York City event or even an event that
happened in the United States. It's an international event. It
connected all victims of terrorism. As I traveled around the
world and I heard other victims talk, 9/11 gave them a voice.
Whether it's London, Madrid, Afghanistan, Israel,
India—every part of the world suffers some sort of terrorist
event. I think the anniversary is a time for people to think
about what took place but also to think about how the world
community can change and can fight terrorism. It's the world
community coming together and saying, These are acts against
humanity, and we can stop it.' —*Joseph Pfeifer, interviewed by
Kate Pickert, New York City, July 9, 2011*

54

JOSEPH PFEIFER
CHIEF OF COUNTERTERRORISM AND EMERGENCY PREPAREDNESS, NEW YORK CITY FIRE DEPARTMENT
"Many of the firefighters who went up there, it was the last time we
saw them. But they went up. They went up and climbed the narrow stairs to help those
that were in their greatest moment of need."

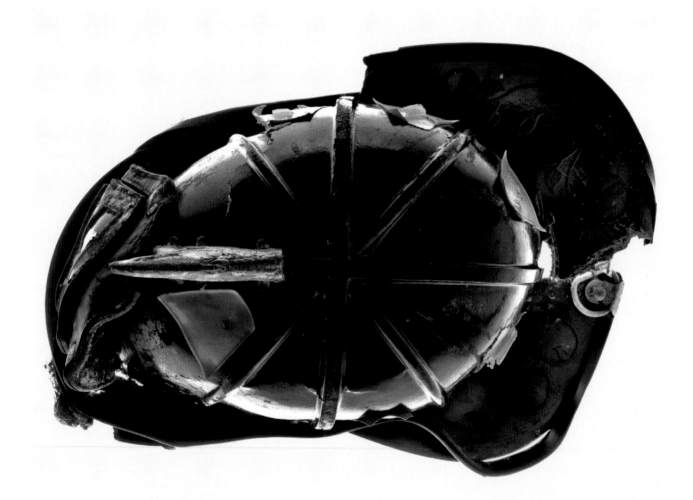

BEYOND 9/11

TOM BROKAW
SPECIAL CORRESPONDENT AND FORMER ANCHOR, NBC NEWS
"What troubles me as much as anything is that I don't think we are still very good at letting people know what the dangers are. The websites of the Department of Homeland Security, the CDC, still are not keeping pace, in my judgment. You ought to be able to go online in a central place, find out what anthrax is, what the effect of it is."

was the police commissioner at the time. He said, "Do you have an assistant that might have had an anthrax lesion of some kind?" And he said, "It's positive. You've had an anthrax attack." It's hard for me to describe, even now, how disorienting it was.

I called Erin immediately. She was very, very upset—with very good reason. She had a small child, had taken a long time to have that child. She was worried about what else may be going on in their household. We didn't know what to do. We learned that one of our interns, Casey Chamberlain, had opened the original letter and dumped out granular brown powder into a wastebasket that had a plastic bag that was sealed off by our maintenance people and disposed of, thank God. The letter that said, "Take penicillin now," we still had, and when the haz-mat crowd from the NYPD came in to test that, it was very hot—and we knew we were in uncharted territory.

Thank God she was on Cipro, so the mass began to shrink. But there was this emotional toll that she was paying. If she could, sitting in my office, be the subject of that kind of attack, what else might happen? At the same time, we were hearing stories about ABC, CBS, the New York Post. It remained a mystery for a long time. The FBI says they've got the guy and that he's the one who committed suicide. He worked at Fort Detrick. What was so stunning to me is we knew so little about biological warfare. We had no real protocol for dealing with it. We couldn't even find out what anthrax looked like. Erin got well eventually. The house was vacated, completely cleaned, sold, and she moved on with her life. But she was the innocent victim of a terrible, evil act.

From a personal point of view, it was the hardest single thing I've ever gone through as a friend, as an employer, even as a journalist. We gave a lot of people Cipro over the course of the next few days, and I remember late in the afternoon on the day that we started to do that, our technical crew—the cameramen and the sound technicians and the stagehands—they'd come in later, they weren't in on it, and they were furious. I went down and talked to them and said, "Look, this is what we know. It's unlikely that you had any exposure, but we're going to get you Cipro right away." When the news ended that night, I said, "I have another way of dealing with this," and I brought out two very large bottles of Jack Daniel's and put them on the desk. "O.K., this is my vaccination against the effects of anthrax. Let's drink up, guys." So we all stood around and had a lot of shooters of Jack Daniel's.

Both from a personal point of view, given what happened in my office, and then widening out the lens to take in all the rest of us, it was a reminder of how important personal relationships are. There was, at the moment of the attacks and in the days afterward, a kind of joining of hearts and minds and will in America, to get through this together. Somehow that's begun to fray, and I think that's sad. I don't think it's a worthy tribute to the people who died, and it ought not to be our legacy. We have to find a way to rekindle that flame. —Tom Brokaw, interviewed by Paul Moakley, New York City, June 24, 2011

26

'I WORKED ALL THE WEEK THROUGH. THERE WAS SO MUCH GOING on—the President with his addresses to the nation, the muster-ing of our military forces that were heading to Afghanistan first, trying to sort out who these hijackers were, hearing the stories of the survivors. I happened to have at that time a great personal assistant, Erin O'Connor, who was the wife of a cop, and her family were firefighters. They were going through their own emotional turmoil—her husband lost a friend at the WTC—but she was very alert to anything that was out of the ordinary. She had gathered a stack of threatening letters and had them off to the side of her desk. She showed me one that said, "Take penicillin now. Death to America. Death to Israel"—very crudely written. Penicillin was misspelled, I remember that.

A couple of days later, Erin said to me, "I've got some kind of a skin inflammation going on." She didn't seem unduly upset by it. She had gone to see a couple of doctors. They weren't sure what it was, but they had started her on Cipro, thank God, which is the antibiotic that you use. By the following Monday, she was in pretty tough shape. I have a friend who is a well-known infectious-diseases expert. We sent her to him the next day, and he was the first one to say to us, "I can't rule out an-thrax." We got biopsies, and we sent them to Fort Detrick, which is the Army installation, and also to the CDC in Atlanta.

On Friday morning I'd gone out for a run early with my dog, and I came back in, and the phone was ringing. I picked it up, and they said, "Commissioner Kerik wants to talk to you." He

ADC

BEYOND 9/11:
PORTRAITS OF RESILIENCE
TIME MAGAZINE
Magazine Editorial | Miscellaneous

DESIGN DIRECTOR: D.W. Pine
SENIOR ART DIRECTOR: Emily Crawford
PHOTOGRAPHER: Marco Grob for TIME
EXECUTIVE PRODUCER: Richard Stengel
PHOTO EDITOR: Erica Fahr Campbell, Caroline Smith, Neil Harris
DEPUTY PHOTO EDITOR: Paul Moakley
CLIENT: TIME Magazine
COUNTRY: United States

'It sounds pretty strange: I'm one of the lucky ones. I found my son's body.'
JIM RICHES
RETIRED DEPUTY
CHIEF, NEW YORK CITY
FIRE DEPARTMENT

From left:
DANNY RICHES
JIM RICHES
TOMMY RICHES
TIMMY RICHES
After their older brother Jimmy's death on Sept. 11, Danny, Tommy and Timmy Riches joined the New York City Fire Department. "I really love working where he worked," Danny says. "I know he'll be supportive of me and proud of me."

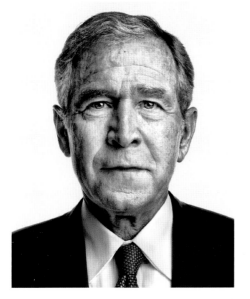

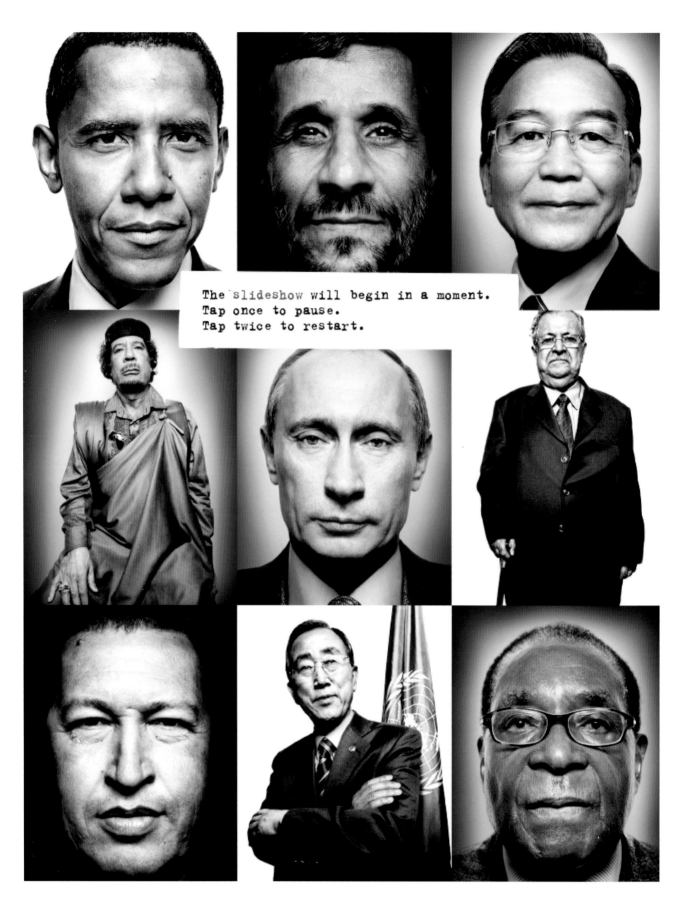

The slideshow will begin in a moment.
Tap once to pause.
Tap twice to restart.

POWER PLATON
EDG, CONDÉ NAST
Magazine Editorial | Miscellaneous

CREATIVE DIRECTOR: Scott Dadich
DESIGNER: Allie Fisher, Victor Krummenacher
ILLUSTRATOR: Yarek Wazul

PHOTOGRAPHER: Platon
CLIENT: Abstract Partners
COUNTRY: United States

"Look into the future and enjoy the ride." Custom-made dress (worn throughout), by special order, **Hussein Chalayan**, 44-207-920-7823. Fashion editor: **Nicola Formichetti**

THE REAL
lady gaga

Be it minimal or maximal, the star's
ICONIC LOOK *comes naturally*

By LAURA BROWN
Photographs by INEZ & VINOODH

A FEW MONTHS AGO, Donatella Versace threw open the doors of the Versace archive in Milan, which contains pieces from the glorious, Medusa'd peak of the Gianni years, for Lady Gaga to plunder at will. "It was me and my friends," Gaga remembers of this particular fashion moment. "We were all running around this warehouse laughing and putting on jackets and shoes. We started crying at one point. I've been dreaming of seeing those outfits my whole life."

It's not a secret that Lady Gaga loves to dress up—in Mugler, in Alexander McQueen, in meat. Lately, "there are some amazing emerging kids from Parsons. I've been wearing a lot of young designers," she explains. She wore ►

276

"I keep in shape by working hard." Hair: Frederic Aspiras for Moroccanoil; makeup: Val Garland.

ADC

THE REAL LADY GAGA
HARPER'S BAZAAR
Magazine Editorial | Fashion

EDITOR IN CHIEF: Glenda Bailey
CREATIVE DIRECTOR: Stephen Gan
DESIGN DIRECTOR: Elizabeth Hummer
DIRECTOR OF PHOTOGRAPHY: Zoe Bruns
PHOTOGRAPHER: Inez & Vinoodh
CLIENT: Harper's Bazaar
COUNTRY: United States

The New York Times Magazine

June 12, 2011

VOYAGES IN AMERICA *A special issue.*

ON EARTH AS IT IS IN HEAVEN
THE NEW YORK TIMES MAGAZINE
Magazine Editorial | Miscellaneous

DESIGN DIRECTOR: Arem Duplessis
ART DIRECTOR: Gail Bichler
DESIGNER: Gail Bichler
DIRECTOR OF PHOTOGRAPHY: Kathy Ryan
PHOTO EDITOR: Luise Stauss
PHOTOGRAPHER: Sebastião Salgado
CLIENT: The New York Times Magazine
COUNTRY: United States

Fifty Million Tourists! Even in bad times, a record year for NYC. Which is ... good? By Michael Idov p.52

Also: Carey Mulligan p.90 / Gary Oldman p.83 / Miranda Kerr p.28 / Rex Ryan p.30

Elena Kagan and 'Obamacare' p.46 / Adventures of an Adderall Pusher p.20

NEW YORK

DECEMBER 5, 2011

TV: What the old, the rich, the young, etc., watch.
PLUS The return of the laugh track. BY JOSEF ADALIAN

Will it be 1968 all over again?

Occupy 2012

BY John Heilemann

$4.99 USA/CANADA
NYMAG.COM
0 74808 01912 0
50

OCCUPY WALL STREET
NEW YORK MAGAZINE
Magazine Editorial | Cover

CHAIRMAN: Adam Moss
ART DIRECTOR: Randy Minor
DIRECTOR OF PHOTOGRAPHY: Jody Quon
PHOTOGRAPHER: Chris Anderson
PHOTO EDITOR: Nadia Lachance
CLIENT: New York Magazine
COUNTRY: United States

JOAN DIDION
NEW YORK MAGAZINE
Magazine Editorial | Miscellaneous

CHAIRMAN: Adam Moss
DIRECTOR OF PHOTOGRAPHY: Jody Quon
PHOTOGRAPHER: Brigitte Lacombe
PHOTO EDITOR: Roxanne Behr
CLIENT: New York Magazine
COUNTRY: United States

THE NEW YORK TIMES MAGAZINE
December 11, 2011

THE HOLLYWOOD ISSUE

with:

JESSICA CHASTAIN
GEORGE CLOONEY
GLENN CLOSE
VIOLA DAVIS
JEAN DUJARDIN
KIRSTEN DUNST
RYAN GOSLING
ROONEY MARA
ADEPERO ODUYE
GARY OLDMAN
BRAD PITT
MICHAEL SHANNON
MIA WASIKOWSKA

VAMPS, CROOKS & KILLERS

THE BEST PERFORMERS FROM THE YEAR IN FILM, RECAST AS NEFARIOUS VILLAINS.

PHOTOGRAPHS BY
ALEX PRAGER

Brad Pitt goes mad!

GEORGE CLOONEY

MIA WASIKOWSKA

GARY OLDMAN

JESSICA CHASTAIN

TOUCH OF EVIL
THE NEW YORK TIMES MAGAZINE
Magazine Editorial | Miscellaneous

DESIGN DIRECTOR: Arem Duplessis
ART DIRECTOR: Gail Bichler
DESIGNER: Hilary Greenbaum
DIRECTOR OF PHOTOGRAPHY: Kathy Ryan
PHOTO EDITOR: Joanna Milter
PHOTOGRAPHER: Alex Prager
PUBLISHER: The New York Times Magazine
CLIENT: The New York Times Magazine
COUNTRY: United States

A SOLDIER'S TRAGEDY
KENJI AOKI PHOTOGRAPHY
Miscellaneous

DESIGN DIRECTOR: D.W. Pine
ART DIRECTOR: Christine Dunleavy
DIRECTOR OF PHOTOGRAPHY: Kira Pollack
PHOTOGRAPHER: Kenji Aoki

PHOTO EDITOR: Crary Pullen
PUBLISHER: TIME Magazine
CLIENT: TIME Magazine
COUNTRY: United States

LONG IS BEAUTIFUL
KENJI AOKI PHOTOGRAPHY
Miscellaneous

CREATIVE DIRECTOR: Javier Bonilla
ART DIRECTOR: Arturo Macouzet,
Mark Cousin
COPYWRITER: Javier Bonilla
PHOTOGRAPHER: Kenji Aoki
PRODUCER: Jayne Horowitz
RETOUCHER: Arturo Macouzet
TYPOGRAPHER: Arturo Macouzet
AGENCY: Wing
CLIENT: Pantene
COUNTRY: United States

LIFE HURTS

★ PROUDLY STANDING IN HARM'S WAY SINCE 1922 ★ *Dickies*

The short sleeve work shirt is moisture-resistant, stain-resistant and hard-luck-resistant.

LIFE HURTS
GOODBY, SILVERSTEIN & PARTNERS
Magazine Advertisement

CHAIRMAN: Rich Silverstein
EXECUTIVE CREATIVE DIRECTOR:
Rich Silverstein, Erik Vervroegen
ART DIRECTOR: Mark Sobier
COPYWRITER: Jonathan Graham
PHOTOGRAPHER: Zach Gold
PRODUCER: Elsbeth Loughrey

PRODUCTION COMPANY:
Copperwind Productions
RETOUCHER: DMAX Imaging
ACCOUNT DIRECTOR: Mark Miller
ART BUYER: Britt Gardner
CLIENT: Dickies
COUNTRY: United States

theshipsongproject.com

THE SHIP SONG PROJECT
MONKEY ONE LLC
Poster or Billboard Advertisement

EXECUTIVE CREATIVE DIRECTOR: Justin Drape   PRODUCTION COMPANY: POOL Productions
CREATIVE DIRECTOR: Noah Regan   RETOUCHER: Cream Studios
ART DIRECTOR: Noah Regan   ART BUYER: Alice Quiddinton
DESIGNER: Noah Regan   AGENCY: The Monkeys
PHOTOGRAPHER: Simon Harsent   CLIENT: Sydney Opera House
EXECUTIVE PRODUCER: Cameron Gray   COUNTRY: Australia

**CONDUCTORS OF THE
MOVING WORLD**
HANS SEEGER
Book

ART DIRECTOR: Hans Seeger
PHOTOGRAPHER: Eizo Ota
PUBLISHER: Little Brown Mushroom Books
CURATOR: Brad Zellar
CLIENT: Little Brown Mushroom Books
COUNTRY: United States

THE POWDER
HANS SEEGER
Book

ART DIRECTOR: Hans Seeger
PHOTOGRAPHER: Various
PUBLISHER: Dashwood Books
CURATOR: Jocko Weyland
CLIENT: Dashwood Books
COUNTRY: United States

"MICHAEL SCHNABEL 2001-2010"
MICHAEL SCHNABEL | PHOTOGRAPHY
Book

DESIGNER: Kirsten Dietz
PHOTOGRAPHER: Michael Schnabel
RETOUCHER:
recom ART + etizy digital artwork
AGENCY: Strichpunkt
CLIENT: Michael Schnabel
COUNTRY: Germany

TABLE PORTRAITS
PETER ROSS
Self-Promotion

DESIGNER: Jennifer Lee
PHOTOGRAPHER: Peter Ross
AGENCY: VSA Partners
COUNTRY: United States

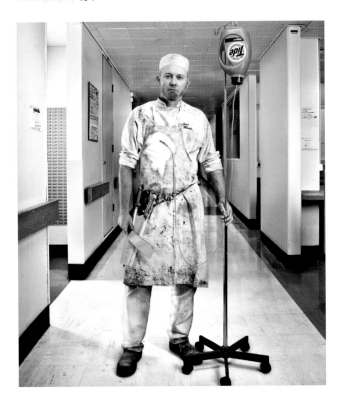

TRANSFUSION
LEO BURNETT SYDNEY
Magazine Advertisement

CHIEF CREATIVE OFFICER: Andy DiLallo
ART DIRECTOR: A. Chris Moreira,
Mark Schöller
COPYWRITER: A. Chris Moreira,
Mark Schöller
PHOTOGRAPHER: Sean Izzard
RETOUCHER: Cream Studios, Sydney
CLIENT: Procter & Gamble
COUNTRY: Australia

ONE ARM
LEO BURNETT SYDNEY
Poster or Billboard Advertisement

CHIEF CREATIVE OFFICER: Andy DiLallo
CREATIVE DIRECTOR: Tim Green
ART DIRECTOR: Tim Green,
Rupert Taylor
COPYWRITER: Rupert Taylor,
Tim Green
PHOTOGRAPHER: Jean-Yves Lemoigne
TYPOGRAPHER: Stuart Tobin
ACCOUNT DIRECTOR: Jodi McLeod
ART BUYER: Gary Clarke
CLIENT: Procter & Gamble
COUNTRY: Australia

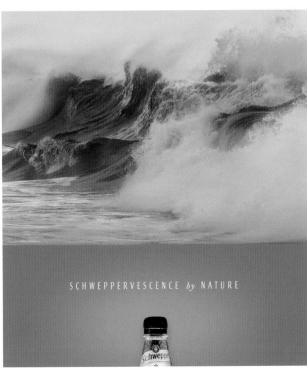

SCHWEPPERVESCENCE BY NATURE
MONKEY ONE LLC
Poster or Billboard Advertisement

EXECUTIVE CREATIVE DIRECTOR:
Ben Coulson
CREATIVE DIRECTOR: Ant Simmons
SENIOR ART DIRECTOR: Fran Webb
COPYWRITER: Annie Egan
PHOTOGRAPHER: Simon Harsent
EXECUTIVE PRODUCER: Cameron Gray
PRODUCER: Stephanie Cohen
PRODUCTION COMPANY: POOL Productions
ACCOUNT DIRECTOR: Courtney Robertson
ART BUYER: Tina Ferreira
AGENCY: GPY&R
CLIENT: Schweppes
COUNTRY: Australia

Photography
Merits

OCCUPY WALL STREET
NEW YORK MAGAZINE
Magazine Editorial | Miscellaneous

CHAIRMAN: Adam Moss
ART DIRECTOR: Randy Minor
DIRECTOR OF PHOTOGRAPHY: Jody Quon
PHOTOGRAPHER: Chris Anderson
PHOTO EDITOR: Nadia Lachance
CLIENT: New York Magazine
COUNTRY: United States

YOUR RENEWABLE ENERGY PLAN
REAL SIMPLE MAGAZINE
Magazine Editorial | Healthcare

CREATIVE DIRECTOR: Janet Froelich
DESIGN DIRECTOR: Cybele Grandjean
ART DIRECTOR: Abbey Kuster-Prokell
DESIGNER: Cybele Grandjean
DIRECTOR OF PHOTOGRAPHY: Casey Tierney
PHOTOGRAPHER: Rodney Smith
PHOTO EDITOR: Brian Madigan
CLIENT: Real Simple Magazine
COUNTRY: United States

MOTHERS OVER 50
NEW YORK MAGAZINE
Magazine Editorial | Cover

CHAIRMAN: Adam Moss
DESIGN DIRECTOR: Chris Dixon
ILLUSTRATOR: Darrow
DIRECTOR OF PHOTOGRAPHY: Jody Quon
PHOTOGRAPHER: Danny Kim
PHOTO EDITOR: Lea Golis
CLIENT: New York Magazine
COUNTRY: United States

SURFRIDER
LEO BURNETT SYDNEY
Poster or Billboard Advertisement

CHIEF CREATIVE OFFICER: Andy DiLallo
CREATIVE DIRECTOR: Mark Harricks
ART DIRECTOR: Brendan Donnelly
COPYWRITER: Guy Futcher
PHOTOGRAPHER: Adam Taylor
ART BUYER: Bryan Holt, Fiona Watson
CLIENT: Surfrider Foundation
COUNTRY: Australia

HOLIDAY FOOD
NEW YORK MAGAZINE
Magazine Editorial | Food

CHAIRMAN: Adam Moss
DIRECTOR OF PHOTOGRAPHY: Jody Quon
PHOTOGRAPHER: Zachary Zavislak
PHOTO EDITOR: Lea Golis
CLIENT: New York Magazine
COUNTRY: United States

VIAREGGIO, ITALY
TOM NAGY
Self-Promotion

PHOTOGRAPHER: Tom Nagy
COUNTRY: Germany

Illustration is tougher than ever.

Keep fighting the good fight.

ArtDirectorsClub

Illustration

The process of looking at so many strong pieces of illustration and design, then deciding what looks and feels the best, was a careful dance. Your mind goes into overdrive going down the list of criteria that the Art Directors Club upholds and represents and what we as judges carry. When it is all complete, you hope that what has survived looks great today, tomorrow and beyond.

Rodrigo Corral
Illustration Jury Chair

Illustration
Jury

Rodrigo
Corral
Farrar, Straus and Giroux
Rodrigo Corral Design
United States

Nicholas
Blechman
The New York Times Book Review
United States

Joel
Holland
Joel Holland Illustration
United States

Chris
Silas Neal
Studio of Chris Silas Neal
United States

Rich
Tu
Rich Tu Design, Pozzle LLC
United States

Marion Deuchars

LET'S MAKE some GREAT ART

Illustration **114**

MATISSE

HENRI MATISSE WAS BORN IN FRANCE IN 1869.
MATISSE IS KNOWN FOR WORK USING EXTRA-
ORDINARY BOLD COLOURS.
AFTER AN ART SHOW IN 1905, CRITICS
STARTED CALLING HIM A 'FAUVE'. THIS MEANS
'WILD BEAST' IN FRENCH!

WHEN HE WAS OLDER, MATISSE'S HEALTH
BEGAN TO FAIL. CONFINED TO A WHEELCHAIR,
HE STARTED MAKING 'COLLAGES' IN A TECHNIQUE
HE CALLED 'Painting with scissors'.

MAKE YOUR OWN MATISSE -
INSPIRED COLLAGE.

WHAT YOU WILL NEED.

A PENCIL
1 SHEET WHITE PAPER
1 SMALLER SQUARE OF COLOURED PAPER
(OR COLOUR YOUR OWN, BOTH SIDES,
WITH PAINT BRUSH OR ROLLER.)
GLUE
SCISSORS

DRAW SOME SHAPES IN PENCIL AND
THEN CUT THEM OUT FROM THE
EDGES OF THE COLOURED SQUARE PAPER

ONCE YOU HAVE CUT OUT ALL YOUR SHAPES
STICK THE REMAINING SQUARE PAPER
WITH GLUE ONTO THE LARGER WHITE
PAPER.

NOW FLIP OVER THE SHAPES YOU HAVE CUT
OUT AND GLUE THEM NEXT TO THE SPACES
THEY WERE CUT FROM TO MAKE POSITIVE/NEGATIVE SHAPES

SEE HOW THE WHITE (NEGATIVE) SPACE
IS JUST AS IMPORTANT AS THE (POSITIVE) COLOURED SHAPES.

FLIP OVER

MATISSE-INSPIRED COLLAGE.

EXPERIMENT FURTHER BY USING TWO COLOURED
SQUARES, OR CHANGE THE BACKGROUND WHITE
PAPER TO A CONTRASTING COLOUR

LET'S MAKE SOME GREAT ART
LAURENCE KING PUBLISHING
Book

ART DIRECTOR: Angus Hyland (Pentagram Design)
ILLUSTRATOR: Marion Deuchars
HEAD OF PRODUCTION: Felicity Awdry
PUBLISHER: Laurence King Publishing
CLIENT: Laurence King Publishing
COUNTRY: United Kingdom

DESIGN | Book Design | Children's Book

AFRICAN MASK

Some of Picasso's
Art was influenced
by African Art which
helped create CUBISM.

FOLD A PIECE OF PAPER
IN HALF AND PAINT HALF
A FACE ON ONE SIDE.
PRESS TOGETHER WHILE
THE PAINT IS STILL WET.
AND OPEN CAREFULLY.

FOLD
HERE ⟶ AND PRESS

African Masks can
be made from wood,
bronze, copper, straw,
ceramic and textiles.
Many represent
animals and are
very colourful.

LAPIS (BLUE) LAZULI

THE RENAISSANCE MASTERS CRUSHED
LAPIS LAZULI ROCKS INTO POWDER
AND MIXED IT WITH OIL TO MAKE AN
INTENSE BLUE.
MANY PAINTINGS OF THE 'MADONNA'
USE THIS PIGMENT.

ROCK POWDER

DURING THE Renaissance
LAPIZ LAZULI WAS MORE
EXPENSIVE THAN GOLD

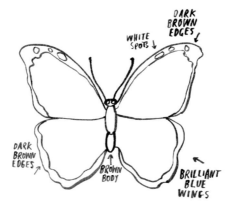

DARK BROWN EDGES

WHITE SPOTS

DARK BROWN EDGES

BROWN BODY

BRILLIANT BLUE WINGS

COLOUR IN THIS BLUE
MORPHO BUTTERFLY

The New York Times Magazine

November 13, 2011

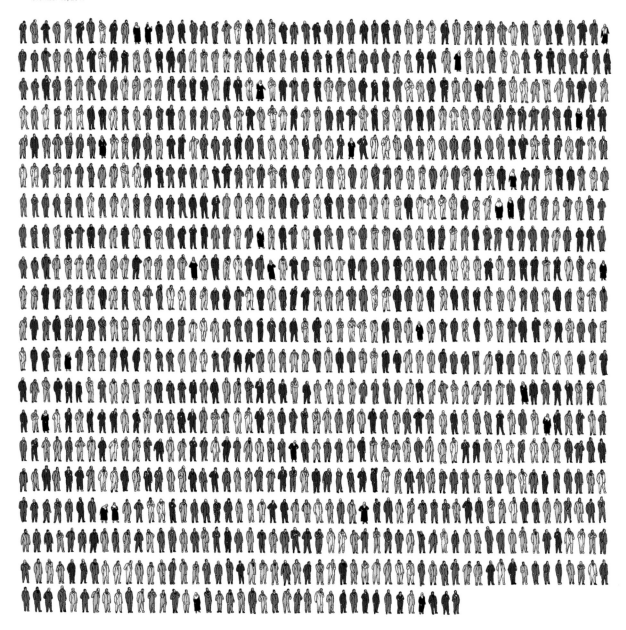

The Human Swap How a single Israeli came to be worth 1,027 Palestinians. By Ronen Bergman

THE HUMAN SWAP
THE NEW YORK TIMES MAGAZINE
Magazine Editorial | Cover

DESIGN DIRECTOR: Arem Duplessis
ART DIRECTOR: Gail Bichler
DESIGNER: Arem Duplessis
ILLUSTRATOR: Tim Enthoven
PUBLISHER: The New York Times Magazine
CLIENT: The New York Times Magazine
COUNTRY: United States

Illustration **116**

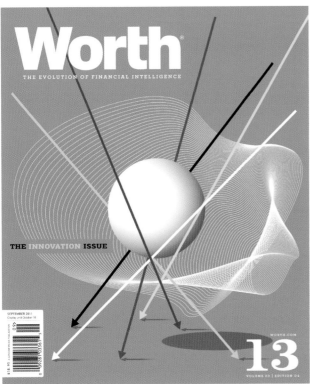

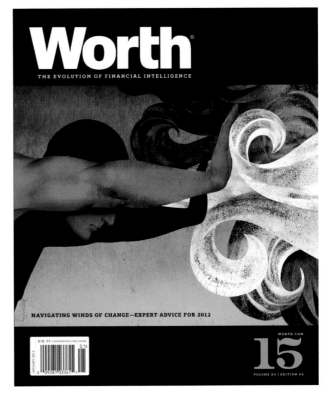

WORTH MAGAZINE COVER SERIES
BRIAN STAUFFER ILLUSTRATION/
LOG CABIN STUDIO
Magazine Editorial | Cover

CREATIVE DIRECTOR: Dean Sebring
ILLUSTRATOR: Brian Stauffer
CLIENT: Worth Magazine
COUNTRY: United States

IMAGINE THE POSSIBILITIES
MAGPIE STUDIO
Poster or Billboard

CREATIVE DIRECTOR: David Azurdia,
Ben Christie, Jamie Ellul
ART DIRECTOR: David Azurdia
DESIGNER: David Azurdia
ILLUSTRATOR: David Azurdia
TYPOGRAPHER: David Azurdia
CLIENT: Robert Horne Group
COUNTRY: United Kingdom

Illustration **118**

WHAT'S IN A BEARD PRINT CAMPAIGN
BBDO NEW YORK
Newspaper Advertisement

EXECUTIVE CREATIVE DIRECTOR:
Toygar Bazarkaya
CHIEF CREATIVE OFFICER: David Lubars
CREATIVE DIRECTOR: Raj Kamble, Paul Vinod
ART DIRECTOR: Raj Kamble
COPYWRITER: Paul Vinod
ILLUSTRATOR: Brosmind
ACCOUNT DIRECTOR: Henrie Clarke,
Cassi Pires, Stephanie Petta
ART BUYER: Sara Gold
CLIENT: Procter & Gamble/
Gillette Fusion ProGlide
COUNTRY: United States

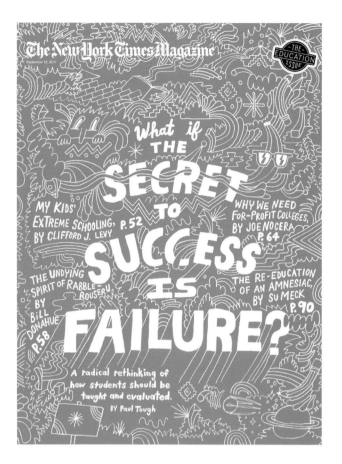

**WHAT IF THE SECRET TO SUCCESS
IS FAILURE?**
THE NEW YORK TIMES MAGAZINE
Magazine Editorial | Cover

DESIGN DIRECTOR: Arem Duplessis
SENIOR ART DIRECTOR: Gail Bichler
ART DIRECTOR: Caleb Bennett
DESIGNER: Drea Zlanabitnig
ILLUSTRATOR: Will Bryant, Dan Cassaro
DIRECTOR OF PHOTOGRAPHY: Kathy Ryan
PUBLISHER: The New York Times Magazine
CLIENT: The New York Times Magazine
COUNTRY: United States

**MUSEUM OF COMMUNISM
GIFT SHOP**
Y&R PRAGUE
Poster or Billboard

CHIEF CREATIVE OFFICER: Jaime Mandelbaum
CREATIVE DIRECTOR: Jaime Mandelbaum
HEAD OF ART: Marco Antonio do Nascimento
ART DIRECTOR: Thiago Jacon
COPYWRITER: Conor Barry
ILLUSTRATOR: Rafael Silveira
CLIENT: Museum of Communism
COUNTRY: Czech Republic

Illustration **120**

**H.O.T
(HOLISTIC ORGANIC TEMPTATION)**
JUNGYEON ROH
Cartoon/Comic Book

ART DIRECTOR: David Sandlin, Josh Cochran
DESIGNER: Jungyeon Roh
ILLUSTRATOR: Jungyeon Roh
TYPOGRAPHER: Jungyeon Roh
CLIENT: School of Visual Arts, Jungyeon Roh
COUNTRY: United States

STEPHEN WILTSHIRE BILLBOARD
PUBLICIS NEW YORK
Poster or Billboard Advertisement

WORLDWIDE CREATIVE DIRECTOR:
Paul Steentjes
EXECUTIVE CREATIVE DIRECTOR:
Jay Williams
ART DIRECTOR: Hajime Ando
COPYWRITER: Jason Savage
ILLUSTRATOR: Stephen Wiltshire
ACCOUNT DIRECTOR: Don Blashford
ART BUYER: Veronica Williams
CLIENT: UBS
COUNTRY: United States

Illustration Merits

Illustration **122**

SOCIAL MEDIA HABITS
MAGNET REPS
Magazine Editorial | Miscellaneous

CREATIVE DIRECTOR: Janet Froelich
ART DIRECTOR: Joele Cuyler
COPYWRITER: Amy Maclin
DESIGNER: Joele Cuyler
ILLUSTRATOR: Graham Roumieu
CLIENT: Real Simple
COUNTRY: United States

HOW TO MAGAZINE –
ILLUSTRATION SERIES
"SHOPPER MARKETING"
OGILVY & MATHER
WERBEAGENTUR GMBH
Corporate/Institutional

CHAIRMAN: Delle Krause
CHIEF EXECUTIVE OFFICER: Thomas Strerath
CREATIVE DIRECTOR: Helmut Meyer,
Delle Krause
DESIGN DIRECTOR: Helmut Meyer
ART DIRECTOR: Helmut Meyer,
Catrin Farrenschon
ILLUSTRATOR: Doc Robert
PRODUCER: Bianca Elbert
PHOTO EDITOR: Alexander Pfaff,
Johanna Woetzel
RETOUCHER: Peter Belz, Joachim Becker
PROJECT MANAGER: Jonas Bailly
ART BUYER: Nathalie Schulz
CLIENT: Ogilvy Germany
COUNTRY: Germany

VIVID LIVE 2011
LA BOCA LTD
Poster or Billboard

ART DIRECTOR: Scot Bendall
ILLUSTRATOR: Scot Bendall, Richard Carey
CURATOR:
Stephen Pavlovic (Modular Records)
CLIENT: The Sydney Opera House
COUNTRY: United Kingdom

THE WORLD OF VOTING MAP
LEO BURNETT TORONTO
Miscellaneous

CHIEF CREATIVE OFFICER: Judy John
CREATIVE DIRECTOR: Judy John,
Lisa Greenberg, Shirley Ward-Taggart
ART DIRECTOR: David Federico, Scott Leder,
Mike Morelli, Matthew Kenney, Ron Cueto,
Brendan Good
COPYWRITER: Morgan Kurchak, Josh Rachlis,
Len Preskow, Joy Panday
DESIGNER: Scott Leder, Chris Duchaine,
Kimberley Pereira, Jeff Watkins, Tracy Ma
ILLUSTRATOR: Chris Duchaine,
Kimberley Pereira, James Joyce
PHOTOGRAPHER: Jesse Senko
PRODUCER: Jacqueline Bellmore
ACCOUNT DIRECTOR: David Buckspan,
Danielle Iozzo, Tara Collins
CLIENT: Elections Ontario
COUNTRY: Canada

HONEY BOND
KOLLE REBBE/KOREFE
Miscellaneous

EXECUTIVE CREATIVE DIRECTOR: Stefan Kolle
CREATIVE DIRECTOR: Antje Hedde,
Katrin Oeding
ART DIRECTOR: Reginald Wagner
COPYWRITER: Gereon Klug,
Moritz Heitmueller
GRAPHIC DESIGNER: Reginald Wagner,
Saara Jaervinen
ILLUSTRATOR: Reginald Wagner
PHOTOGRAPHER: Ulrike Kirmse
PRODUCER: Stephan Gerlach
RETOUCHER: Lea Fechtig
ACCOUNT DIRECTOR: Felix Negwer,
Kristina Wulf
CLIENT: The Deli Garage,
T.D.G. Vertriebs GmbH & Co. KG
COUNTRY: Germany

LET IT BLEND
PERFIL252
Photo-Illustration

CHAIRMAN: Carlos Eduardo Porto Moreno
CHIEF CREATIVE OFFICER: Waldemar França,
Márcia Lima
DESIGN DIRECTOR: Waldemar França
SENIOR ART DIRECTOR: Waldemar França
ART DIRECTOR: Waldemar França
COPYWRITER: Márcia Lima
DESIGNER: Waldemar França
ILLUSTRATOR: Waldemar França
PHOTO EDITOR: Waldemar França
RETOUCHER: Waldemar França
TYPOGRAPHER: Waldemar França,
Rafael Matos
ACCOUNT DIRECTOR: Cristiane Almeida
CLIENT: Xitam Indie Rockband
COUNTRY: Brazil

ICON7 POSTER: DRAWN TOGETHER
CHRIS BUZELLI
Poster or Billboard

CREATIVE DIRECTOR: John Hendrix
ART DIRECTOR: John Hendrix
DESIGNER: Jessica Hische
ILLUSTRATOR: Chris Buzelli
CLIENT: ICON The Illustration: Conference
COUNTRY: United States

MICCHAN
IC4DESIGN
Poster or Billboard Advertisement

CREATIVE DIRECTOR: Maka Kouchi
ART DIRECTOR: Hiro Kamigaki (IC4Design)
ILLUSTRATOR: IC4Design
PRODUCER: Masakazu Ise, Naoya Kobayashi
CLIENT: MICCHAN
COUNTRY: Japan

Motion is tougher than ever.

ArtDirectorsClub

Mo
tion

As this is the first year that Motion Design made an appearance as its own category in the ADC Awards, a tremendous amount of thought went into recognizing a body of work that equaled the design craftsmanship and conceptual prowess of the work in the other categories despite its relative infancy. To that end, I am truly proud to have had judges that represent a diverse cross section of the studios, artists, and thinkers in the field. Together, we were able to help set a new precedent for what can be considered the highest level of creative in a field that is now arguably truly mature.

Andre Stringer
Motion Jury Chair

Motion Jury

Andre Stringer
Andre Stringer TV
United States

Greg Brunkalla
Artists and Derelicts
United States

Justin Cone
Motiongrapher
United States

Gerald Soto
Salvame,
geraldmarksoto.com
United States

Orion Tait
Buck
United States

CHIPOTLE'S BACK TO THE START
CREATIVE ARTISTS AGENCY
AND CHIPOTLE
Broadcast Craft | Animation

DIRECTOR: Johnny Kelly
PRODUCER: Liz Chan
PRODUCTION COMPANY: Nexus Productions
MUSIC SUPERVISION: David Leinheardt
(Duotone Audio Group)
MUSIC PRODUCER: Justin Stanley,
Doyle Bramhall
SONG: Willie Nelson covering Coldplay's
"The Scientist"
CONTENT MANAGER: Liz Graves
CLIENT: Chipotle
COUNTRY: United States

DESIGNISM

DESIGN | Motion | Animation
DESIGN | Motion | Direction
INTERACTIVE | Online Content |
Original Web Commercials

ADVERTISING | TV/Film
Cinema Commercial
ADVERTISING | Broadcast Craft |
Art Direction

DUOTONE AUDIO GROUP
ADVERTISING | Broadcast Craft |
Television Music/Sound Design

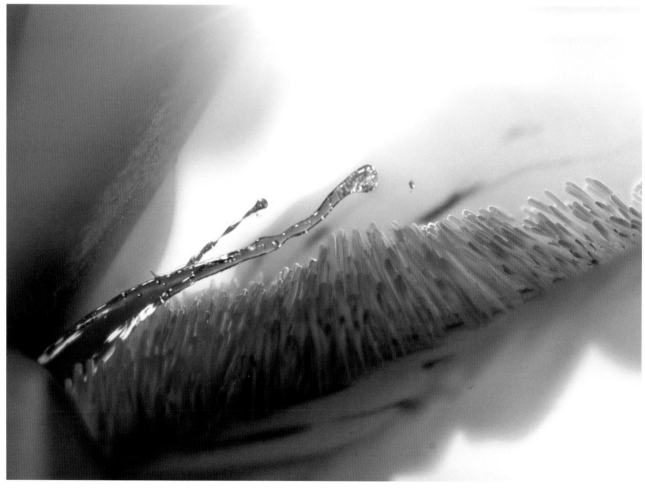

PLAIN
MULLEN
Cinematography

CHIEF CREATIVE OFFICER: Mark Wenneker
CREATIVE DIRECTOR: Brian Tierney
DESIGN DIRECTOR: Kevin Grady
ART DIRECTOR: Kevin Grady
COPYWRITER: Brian Tierney
DIRECTOR OF PHOTOGRAPHY: Christopher Doyle
ANIMATOR: Psyop, New York
DIRECTOR: Psyop, New York
EDITOR: Vico Sharabani, El Ohayan
HEAD OF PRODUCTION: Lucia Grillo
EXECUTIVE PRODUCER: Lucia Grillo
PRODUCER: Carol Collins
LINE PRODUCER: Karen O'Brien
PRODUCTION COMPANY: Psyop, Smuggler
VISUAL EFFECTS: Psyop, New York
SOUND DESIGN: Pivot Audio
MUSIC/COMPOSER: Guy Amitai
CLIENT: FAGE
COUNTRY: United States

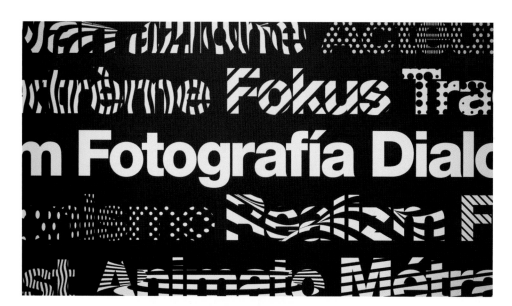

CRITICS CHOICE MOVIE AWARDS
GRETEL
TV Identities/Openings/Teasers

EXECUTIVE CREATIVE DIRECTOR: Greg Hahn
CREATIVE DIRECTOR: Ryan Moore
DESIGNER: Ryan Moore, Dylan Mulvaney,
Carl Burton
ANIMATOR: Irene Park, Carl Burton,
Bryan Cobonpue, Wes Ebelhar, Gary Tam,
Daniel Garcia
PRODUCER: Angela Foster
SOUND DESIGN: Echolab
MUSIC/COMPOSER: Gavin Little
CLIENT: Vh1
COUNTRY: United States

MOTION | Motion Graphics

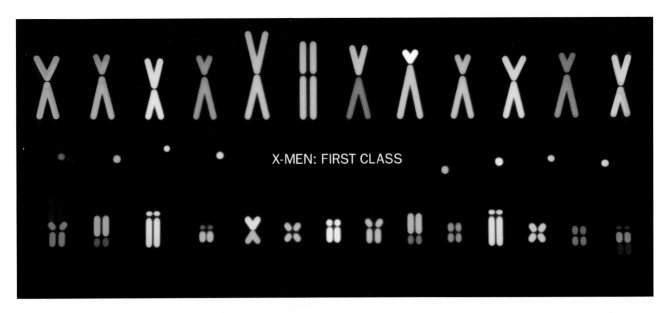

and KEVIN BACON

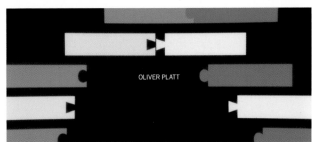

OLIVER PLATT

MICHAEL FASSBENDER

co-producer JASON TAYLOR

associate producer TOM COHEN

executive producers
STAN LEE
TARQUIN PACK
JOSH McLAGLEN

story by
SHELDON TURNER
and BRYAN SINGER

X-MEN: FIRST CLASS
MAIN ON END TITLE SEQUENCE
PROLOGUE FILMS
Title Design

CREATIVE DIRECTOR: Simon Clowes
ANIMATOR: Alasdair JT Wilson
EXECUTIVE PRODUCER: Kyle Cooper
PRODUCER: Unjoo Byars
PRODUCTION COMPANY: Prologue Films
CLIENT: Matthew Vaughn,
Twentieth Century Fox and
Bad Hat Harry Productions
COUNTRY: United States

ENCHANTED FOREST
BBDO NEW YORK
Animation

EXECUTIVE CREATIVE DIRECTOR: Greg Hahn,
Mike Smith
CHIEF CREATIVE OFFICER: David Lubars
CREATIVE DIRECTOR: Tom Kraemer,
Nick Klinkert, Chris Beresford-Hill
ART DIRECTOR: Nick Klinkert
COPYWRITER: Tom Kraemer,
Chris Beresford-Hill
DESIGNER: Lauren Indovina, Jon Saunders,
Naomi Chen
DIRECTOR OF PHOTOGRAPHY: Fredrick Elmes
PHOTOGRAPHER: Jonah Friedman
ANIMATOR: Pat Porter, Amy Hay,
Roman Kobryn, Min Seok Jeon,
Stephanie Russell, Michael Shin
DIRECTOR: Marco Spier, Marie Hyon
EDITOR: Cass Vanini
EXECUTIVE PRODUCER: Lucia Grillo,
Patrick Milling Smith, Brian Carmody, Lisa Rich,
Allison Kunzman, Laura Thoel
PRODUCER: Crystal Campbell, Anu Nagaraj,
Donald Taylor
PRODUCTION COMPANY: Psyop, Smuggler
VISUAL EFFECTS: Dave Barosin,
Miguel Salek (Psyop)
SOUND DESIGN: Sound Lounge
MUSIC/COMPOSER:
Matthew O'Malley (Human)
ACCOUNT DIRECTOR: Lorri Esnard,
Peter McCallum, Julie Meyerson,
Catherine Cyr, Caroline Creek
CLIENT: FedEx
COUNTRY: United States

GOALS
LOBO
Art Direction

CREATIVE DIRECTOR: Guto Terni,
Nando Cohen, Roberto Fernandez
ART DIRECTOR: Filipe Cuvero
COPYWRITER: Christian Fontana
ANIMATOR: Helio Takahashi,
Jason Tadeu Oliveira, Aulo Licino,
Guilherme Gubert
EXECUTIVE PRODUCER: Alberto Lopes,
Sérgio Salles
RTV PRODUCER: Renata Sayão, Daniele Pizzo,
Vanessa Nunes
DIRECTOR COMPANY: Vetor Zero & Animatorio
SOUND DESIGN: YB Music, Anvil Fx/Afroreggea
ACCOUNT MANAGEMENT: Roberta Reigado,
Renata Maximo, Ana Hernandes, Isabel Castro
MEDIA: Ezra Geld, David Ralitera
CHARACTER DEVELOPER: Marcos Felix,
Fernando Cintra, Manuel Augusto Dischinger
CONCEPTS: Manuel Augusto Dischinger,
Ernesto Issamu, Davi Calil
STORYBOARD: Davi Calil
COORDINATION: Valeria Souza Santos
CG SUPERVISOR: Fábio Shiguemura, Tiago Dias
3-D COORDINATOR: Cristiane Santos
MODELING: Filipe Lopes, Rafael Ghencev,
Daniel Ho Ito, Danilo Enoki, Daniel Adami,
Guga Certain, Iara Furuse Abigalil,
Marcos Smirkoff
RIGGING: Richard Maegeki, Danilo Pinheiro,
Wesley Schneider, Vivi Adade
SCRIPT: Giovani Menegel, Rogerio Miyagi
PARTICLES: Cristian Lucas
RENDERING: Tiago Dias, Rafael Martinez,
Ricardo Riamonde
COMPOSITION: Tiago Dias, Bruno Ferrari
FLAME: José Eduardo Ambrósio
CLIENT APPROVAL: Jonathan Lawlor,
Luciana Feres, Ana Paula Castelo Branco,
Patricia Esteves, Ricardo Scorzelli,
Gian Martinez, Paloma Azulay, Marry Zek,
Ana Franklin
REGENT: Anvil Fx
PLANNING: Fernand Alphen
AGENCY: JWT Sao Paulo
CLIENT: Coca-Cola
COUNTRY: Brazil

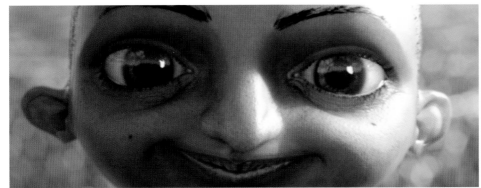

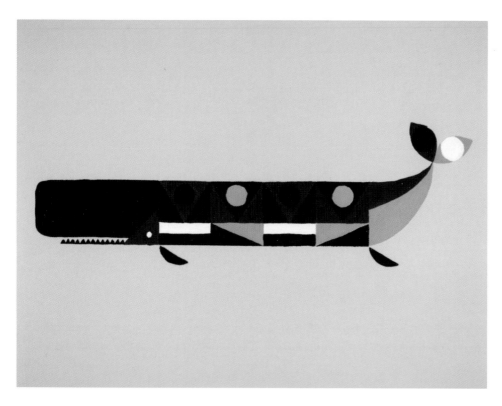

F5 – OPENING TITLES
BUCK
Direction

CREATIVE DIRECTOR: Orion Tait
ART DIRECTOR: Gareth O'Brien, Yker Moreno,
Daniel Oeffinger, Thomas Schmid
DESIGNER: Yker Moreno, Chad Colby,
Thomas Schmid, Daniel Oeffinger, Chris Phillips
COLORIST: Seth Ricart
DIRECTOR OF PHOTOGRAPHY: Seth Ricart
ANIMATOR: Daniel Oeffinger
ANIMATION/ COMPOSITE: Chad Colby,
Yker Moreno, Chris Phillips
DIRECTOR: Buck
EXECUTIVE PRODUCER: Anne Skopas
PRODUCER: Kitty Dillard
PRODUCTION COORDINATOR: Billy Mack
AUDIO: Antfood
SCRIPT: Gareth O'Brien, Victoria Grant
SET DESIGN: Gareth O'Brien
PUPPET DESIGN: Gareth O'Brien
SET CONSTRUCTION: Gareth O'Brien,
Victoria Grant, Kitty Dillard, Andreas Berglund
PUPPET CONSTRUCTION: Tim Lagasse,
Victoria Grant, Gareth O'Brien
STORYBOARDS: Gareth O'Brien
EDIT/COMPOSITE: Gareth O'Brien,
Justin Lawes
SIR BASIL MYRTLE WILLOUGHBY (CHARACTER):
Tim Lagasse
NOODLES (CHARACTER): James Godwin
CHARACTER FACES: Victoria Grant,
Enricco Contreras, Andreina Restrepo,
Waleed Zaiter, Saadia Shiina,
Justin Lawes, Chad Colby
PROPS: Confetti System
PAINTING: Thomas Schmid, Justin Lawes,
Maceo Frost, Andreas Berglund, Kitty Dillard,
Anne Skopas
COMPOSITE: Daniel Oeffinger, Maceo Frost
VOICE TALENT: Jude Tait,
Griffin Van Rhyn
BLOW DART CONSTRUCTION:
Daniel Oeffinger, Soomin Baik
CLIENT: F5
COUNTRY: United States

7TV REBRANDING IDENTS
GREG BARTH
TV Identities/Openings/Teasers

CHAIRMAN: Greg Barth
CREATIVE DIRECTOR: Greg Barth
DESIGN DIRECTOR: Greg Barth
SENIOR ART DIRECTOR: Greg Barth
ART DIRECTOR: Greg Barth
DESIGNER: Jeremy Dabrowski, Julie Ledru
DIRECTOR OF PHOTOGRAPHY: Noé Sardet
ANIMATOR: Clement Yeh, Ian Langhor,
Guillaume Kukucka,
Charlotte Beadouin-Pelletier, Xavier Ferrero,
Florian Golay, Julie Ledru, Alex da Cunha,
Greg Barth, Noé Sardet, Sylvain Lavoie,
Patrick Rochon, Jason Harvey, Naim Jean-Bart

DIRECTOR: Greg Barth
HEAD OF PRODUCTION: Sylvain Lavoie
PRODUCER: Noe Sardet
VISUAL EFFECTS: Robert Quinn
SOUND DESIGN: Nookaad Productions
MUSIC/COMPOSER: Nookaad Productions
PHOTO EDITOR: Maxime Roux
RETOUCHER: Maxime Roux
PROJECT MANAGER: Colas Wohlfahrt
ACCOUNT DIRECTOR: Greg Barth
CLIENT: 7TV
COUNTRY: Canada

IBM WINTER 2011
PSYOP
Animation

EXECUTIVE CREATIVE DIRECTOR:
Susan Westre
CHIEF CREATIVE OFFICER: Steve Simpson
CREATIVE DIRECTOR: Mike Hahn, Ryan Blank
ART DIRECTOR: Jillian Abramson
COPYWRITER: Fred Kovey, Andrew Mellen
DIRECTOR: Psyop
EDITOR: Cass Vanini, Jonathan Flaum
EXECUTIVE PRODUCER: Lee Weiss
PRODUCER: Crystal Campbell
PRODUCTION COMPANY:
Psyop/Smuggler, New York
VISUAL EFFECTS: Psyop, New York
SOUND DESIGN: Pulse Music
MUSIC/COMPOSER: Jason Lifton, Dan Kuby
AGENCY: Ogilvy & Mather New York
CLIENT: IBM
COUNTRY: United States

STUFF
BBDO NEW YORK
Animation

CHIEF CREATIVE OFFICER: David Lubars
CREATIVE DIRECTOR: Linda Honan
ART DIRECTOR: Kim Haxton
COPYWRITER: Nick Sonderup, Ginger Robinson
DESIGNER: Henry De Leon
ANIMATOR: Frantz Vidal, Matt Ornstein,
Pablo Smith, Lindsey Butterworth
DIRECTOR: Andy Hall
EXECUTIVE PRODUCER: Jennifer Sofio Hall
PRODUCER: Heather Johann
PRODUCTION COMPANY: Elastic
SOUND DESIGN: POP Sound
MUSIC/COMPOSER: Search Party,
Mark Mothersbaugh (Mutato Muzika)
CLIENT: American Red Cross
COUNTRY: United States

GOOGLE OFFERS
BUCK
Animation

EXECUTIVE CREATIVE DIRECTOR:
Ryan Honey
CREATIVE DIRECTOR: Jeremy Sahlman,
Joshua Harvey
ART DIRECTOR: Joe Mullen
COPYWRITER: Ryan Honey, Joe Mullen,
Jeremy Sahlman, Andy Kadin
DESIGNER: Joe Mullen
ANIMATOR: Buck
DIRECTOR: Buck
EXECUTIVE PRODUCER: Maurie Enochson
PRODUCER: Eric Badros
PRODUCTION COMPANY: Buck
VISUAL EFFECTS: Buck
SOUND DESIGN: Antfood
MUSIC/COMPOSER: Antfood
PROJECT MANAGER: Julia Tang,
David Kim (Google)
CLIENT: Google
COUNTRY: United States

GET READY
MIRADA
Editing

CHAIRMAN: Michael D'Antonio
CREATIVE DIRECTOR: Parag Tembulkar,
Craig Smith
SENIOR ART DIRECTOR: Jonathan Wu
ART DIRECTOR: Craig Smith
COPYWRITER: Parag Tembulkar
DESIGNER: Chris Ballard
DIRECTOR OF PHOTOGRAPHY: Eric Schmidt
ANIMATOR: Phil Guthrie, Thomas Horne,
Ed Laag, Jason Lowe, Oliver Scott,
Ash Wagers
DIRECTOR: Mark Kudsi
LEAD EDITOR: Lenny Mesina
ADDITIONAL EDITING: Fred Fouquet

EXECUTIVE PRODUCER: Javier Jimenez
VISUAL EFFECTS PRODUCER: James Taylor
LINE PRODUCER: Anna Joseph
PRODUCTION COMPANY:
MTh (Motion Theory)
VISUAL EFFECTS: Mirada
SOUND DESIGN: The Glitch Mob
MUSIC/COMPOSER: MassiveMusic
RETOUCHER: Danny Yoon, Matt Bramante
PROGRAMMER: Keith Pasko, Tim Stutts
ACCOUNT DIRECTOR: Jason Hayes
AGENCY: Impatto Detroit
CLIENT: Fiat
COUNTRY: United States

A RELENTLESS FORCE
PHILIPP UND KEUNTJE GMBH
Special Effects

CREATIVE DIRECTOR: Diether Kerner,
Sönke Schmidt
ART DIRECTOR: Rouven Steiman
COPYWRITER: Sandra Eichner,
Adrienne Tonner
DIRECTOR OF PHOTOGRAPHY:
Jordan Valenti, Kurt Soderling
DIRECTOR: Ole Peters
EDITOR: Stephan Wever
EXECUTIVE PRODUCER: Martin Woelke
PRODUCER: Andreas Coutsoumbelis,
Jan Tiller
PRODUCTION COMPANY: Sehsucht Hamburg
VISUAL EFFECTS: Timo von Wittken,
Florian Zachau
SOUND DESIGN: Supreme Music
MUSIC/COMPOSER:
Ian O´Brien-Docker, Sebastian Zenke
ACCOUNT DIRECTOR: Steffen Schwab
CLIENT: Automobili Lamborghini S.p.A.
COUNTRY: Germany

Motion
Merits

APPLES
LEO BURNETT CHICAGO
Animation

EXECUTIVE CREATIVE DIRECTOR:
John Montgomery
CHIEF CREATIVE OFFICER: Susan Credle
CREATIVE DIRECTOR: Keith Hughes
ART DIRECTOR: Keith Hughes, Trip Park
COPYWRITER: Susan Credle,
John Montgomery
ANIMATOR: Laszlo Nyikos, Gabor Lendvai
DIRECTOR: Oliver Conrad
EXECUTIVE PRODUCER: Mark Medernach,
Gian Klainguti
PRODUCER: Eric Faber
PRODUCTION COMPANY: Duck Studios, Kompost
VISUAL EFFECTS: Kenneth Polonski,
Christopher Soyer
SOUND DESIGN: Bonny Dolan (Comma)
MUSIC/COMPOSER: Justin Roberts
SONG: Apple Tree
PROJECT MANAGER: Araya Berhard
ACCOUNT DIRECTOR: Bob Ferdman,
Jenny Cacioppo
CLIENT: McDonald's
COUNTRY: United States

MITE CITY
KOLLE REBBE
Animation

EXECUTIVE CREATIVE DIRECTOR:
Stefan Wuebbe
CREATIVE DIRECTOR: Thomas Knuewer
ART DIRECTOR: Thomas Knuewer
COPYWRITER: Dennis Krumbe
DESIGNER: Mate Steinforth, Jonas Littke,
Ronny Schmidt, Christian Zschunke
ANIMATOR: Philipp Broemme, Helge Kiehl,
Chris Hoffmann, Philipp Rudler
DIRECTOR: Mate Steinforth
PRODUCER: Bey-Bey Chen (Kolle Rebbe),
Christian Gemenier (Sehsucht)
PRODUCTION COMPANY:
Sehsucht Berlin GmbH & Co. KG
3-D LEAD: Hannes Weikert
SOUND DESIGN: Supreme Music, Hamburg
AUDIO MIX: Studio Funk, Hamburg
ACCOUNT DIRECTOR: Jan Kowalsky
CLIENT: Vorwerk Kobold Deutschland & Co. KG
COUNTRY: Germany

Interactive is tougher than ever.

Keep fighting the good fight.   ArtDirectorsClub

Interactive

This year, the interactive world is richer and more interesting than ever. It's also heartening to see entries with a social conscience. Take 'Back to the Start,' a beautifully crafted piece of content that told a brand story with heart. And who would have questioned the human cost in the everyday we take for granted? The 'Slavery Footprint' did.

Not everything needs to be big. 'Smart-eball' is a well-executed example of real-world interaction and product demonstration, that also manages to transport us back in time—you wanted to be in those seats. Small is the new big. And there is no better exemplar of 'small' than in the craft. 'Wall of Fame' shows us the beauty of the product magnified infinitely in the interactive space.

Congratulations to all.

I'm humbled to be the chair and thankful to the diversely inspiring jury.

Here's to an ever-changing medium, and an even more interesting year ahead!

Natalie Lam
Interactive Jury Chair

Interactive Jury

Natalie Lam
McCann Erickson New York
United States

Wade Convay
R/GA
United States

Mehera O'Brien
Miami Ad School New York
United States

Jens Schmidt
Moccu GmbH & Co. KG
Germany

Christian Ayotte
Sid Lee
Canada

Marta Cutler
Blok Design
Canada

Karin Onsager-Birch
Blue Hive
United Kingdom

Kristina Slade
AKQA
United States

Miguel Calderon
GrupoW
Mexico

David Eveleigh-Evans
Method, Inc.
United Kingdom

Karyn Pascoe
ORGANIC
United States

Oscar Tillman
B-Reel
United States

Belén Coca
La Despensa
Spain

Joshua Hirsch
Big Spaceship
United States

Steve Persico
Leo Burnett Toronto
Canada

James Widegren
Your Majesty
United States

Jacob Cohen
frog design
United States

Dan LaCivita
Firstborn
United States

Malcolm Poynton
SapientNitro
United Kingdom

How many slaves work for you?

What?
Slaves work for me?
↓

Find out
Take the survey
→

You Have

53 Slaves Working For You. Now what?

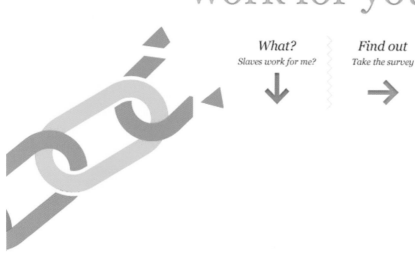

← **My Footprint**

→ **Take Action**

→ **Messages**

→ **Groups**

 Get App
Fight slavery with your phone

Share your results
 Facebook
 Twitter

RT @Slave_Footprint: How ethical is your Easter basket? Tell your favorite chocolate brands you want products #madeinafreeworld http://t.co/NgE6VKWI

How ethical is your Easter basket? Tell your favorite chocolate brands you want products #madeinafreeworld http://t.co/NgE6VKWI

Take Action

The slaves who work for you are all over the world, working the supply chains for the things you use. Your main areas of impact are mapped. Tap a circle to see the number of slaves working for you in that location and how slavery affects raw materials produced there. To start fighting your footprint, go to the Take Action tab, download the app and learn how you can earn Free World points.

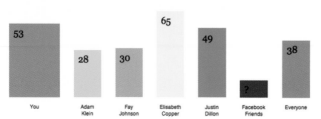

You	Adam Klein	Fay Johnson	Elisabeth Copper	Justin Dillon	Facebook Friends	Everyone
53	28	30	65	49	?	38

SLAVERY FOOTPRINT
MUH•TAY•ZIK | HOF•FER
Website | Campaign Site

EXECUTIVE CREATIVE DIRECTOR:
John Matejczyk
CREATIVE DIRECTOR: Diko Daghlian
DESIGN DIRECTOR: Luciano Foglio
SENIOR ART DIRECTOR: Diko Daghlian
ART DIRECTOR: Omid Rashidi
COPYWRITER: John Matejczyk, Aaron Sanchez,
Mike Gallucci, Melissa Blaser
DESIGNER: Elena Lombardi
ILLUSTRATOR: Elena Lombardi
ANIMATOR: Maki Yoshikura,
Benz Anwat Vongtanee
DIRECTOR: Robert Bader
EXECUTIVE PRODUCER: Michelle Spear,
Emmanuel Saccoccini
PRODUCER: Kelli Bratvold, Mel Di Prinzio
PRODUCTION COMPANY: unit9
PROGRAMMER: Sam Brown, Todd Moore,
Christian Bianchini
ACCOUNT DIRECTOR: Kacine Kromrey
CLIENT: Call & Response and the
U.S. State Department
COUNTRY: United States

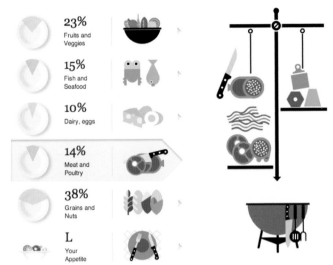

Shrimp Cocktail, Anyone?

Bonded labor is used for much of Southeast Asia's shrimping industry, which supplies more shrimp to the U.S. than any other country. Laborers work up to 20-hour days to peel 40 pounds of shrimp. Those who attempt to escape are under constant threat of violence or sexual assault.

f t 81K

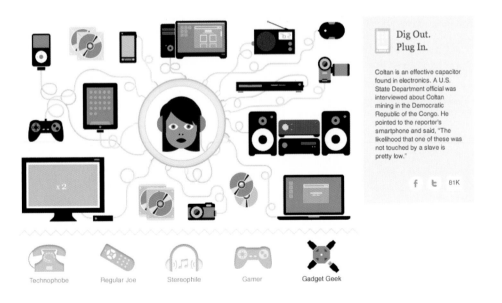

Dig Out. Plug In.

Coltan is an effective capacitor found in electronics. A U.S. State Department official was interviewed about Coltan mining in the Democratic Republic of the Congo. He pointed to the reporter's smartphone and said, "The likelihood that one of these was not touched by a slave is pretty low."

f t 81K

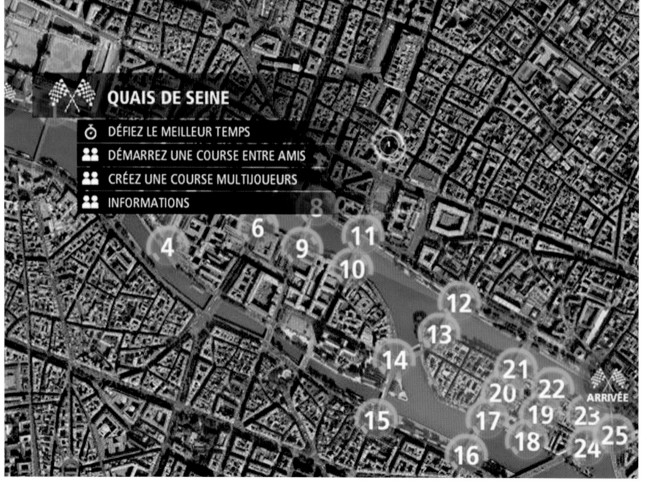

QUAIS DE SEINE

DÉFIEZ LE MEILLEUR TEMPS

DÉMARREZ UNE COURSE ENTRE AMIS

CRÉEZ UNE COURSE MULTIJOUEURS

INFORMATIONS

4 6 8 9 10 11 12 13 14 15 16 17 18 19 20 21 22 23 24 25

ARRIVÉE

MINI MAPS
DDB PARIS
Social | Online Game

CHAIRMAN: Jean-Luc Bravi,
Matthieu de Lesseux
VICE CHAIRMAN: Alexandre Hervé
EXECUTIVE CREATIVE DIRECTOR:
Alexandre Hervé
ART DIRECTOR: Alexis Benbehe,
Pierre Mathonat
COPYWRITER: Alexis Benbehe,
Pierre Mathonat
AGENCY PRODUCER: Guillaume Cossou
PRODUCTION COMPANY: unit9
MOTION DESIGN: Julien Taillez
PROJECT MANAGER: Florent Depoisier,
Paul Royer
ACCOUNT DIRECTOR: Vincent Léorat,
Matthieu Porri
CLIENT: MINI France
COUNTRY: France

WALL OF FAME
KEMPERTRAUTMANN GMBH
Website | Campaign Site

CREATIVE DIRECTOR: Simon-Jasper Philipp,
Christoph Gähwiler, Stefan Walz, Gerrit Zinke
ART DIRECTOR: Simon-Jasper Philipp,
Stefan Walz, Florian Schimmer
COPYWRITER: Christoph Gähwiler,
Samuel Weiß, Michael Götz
DESIGNER: David Scherer, Tobias Lehment
PHOTOGRAPHER: Nordstern Studio
PRODUCTION COMPANY: Liga_01,
demodern| digital design studio
VISUAL EFFECTS: Liga_01.
demodern| digital design studio
SOUND DESIGN: Supreme Music OhG
PHOTO EDITOR: flavouredgreen,
PX Group GmbH
PROGRAMMER:
demodern| digital design studio
CLIENT: edding International GmbH
COUNTRY: Germany

**THINK: AN EXPLORATION INTO
MAKING THE WORLD WORK BETTER**
MIRADA, SYPARTNERS
Physical | Installation

EXECUTIVE CREATIVE DIRECTOR:
Susana Rodriguez de Tembleque,
Nicolas Maitret (SYPartners),
Mathew Cullen (Mirada)
CREATIVE DIRECTOR: Jesus De Francisco,
Kaan Atilla (Mirada)
DESIGN DIRECTOR: James Cathcart
(Ralph Appelbaum Associates, Inc.)
SENIOR ART DIRECTOR: Jonathan Wu (Mirada),
Heui Jin Jo, Becky Hui (SYPartners)
COPYWRITER: Jeff O'Brien, Stuart Luman,
Keith Yamashita, Nicholas Maitret,
Susana Rodriguez de Tembleque, Julie Felner,
Tom Raith (SYPartners), David Fowler (Mirada)
DESIGNER: Mark Brinn, Hye Jung Bae,
Daryn Wakasa, Christopher Ballard, Ivan Cruz,
Luca Giannettoni, Ben Hansford, Jairen Hui,
James Kim, Aaron Lam, James Levy,
Miwa Matreyek, An Nguyen, Jane Ro,
Andrea Tseng, Wilson Wu, Jacklin Yoo (Mirada),
Josh Hartley, Rosanna Vitiello, Carlos Rodriguez,
Andri Klausen (Ralph Appelbaum Associates Inc.)
ILLUSTRATOR: Josh Cochran (Mirada),
Carl DeTorres (SYPartners)
DIRECTOR OF PHOTOGRAPHY:
Guillermo Navarro (MTh (Motion Theory))
ANIMATOR: John Robson, Frank Lin,
Jason Lowe (Mirada)
DIRECTOR: Mathew Cullen
(MTh (Motion Theory))
EDITOR: Lenny Mesina, Fred Fouquet,
Bryan Keith (Mirada)
EXECUTIVE PRODUCER: Javier Jimenez
(MTh (Motion Theory)), Alex Vlack
(Ralph Appelbaum Associates Inc.)
PRODUCER: Annie Johnson
(MTh (Motion Theory)), Lilly Preston
(Ralph Appelbaum Associates, Inc.)
PRODUCTION COMPANY: MTh (Motion Theory)
HEAD OF VISUAL EFFECTS: John Fragomeni
HEAD OF ANIMATION: John Fragomeni
VISUAL EFFECTS SUPERVISORS:
Andy Cochrane, Jonah Hall, Zach Tucker (Mirada)
SOUND DESIGN: Steve Borne
PROGRAMMER: Casey Reas, David Wicks,
Jonathan Cecil, John Houck, Rhazes Spell (Mirada),
Eric Gunther, John Rothenberg,
Justin Manor, Lauren McCarthy (SoSoLimited)
PROJECT MANAGER: Andy Merkin (Mirada),
Sabrina Clark (SYPartners),
Caitlin Mennen-Bobula
(Ralph Appelbaum Associates, Inc.),
Sarah Frantz (George P. Johnson)
AGENCY: MTh (Motion Theory),
Ralph Appelbaum Associates, Inc.,
George P. Johnson
CLIENT: IBM
COUNTRY: United States

ADC AUDIENCE AWARD

THE PONG TEST DRIVE PROJECT

» The first video game in the world that turns electric cars into controllers. And sceptics into fans.

1. CHALLENGE: Electric cars are known to be eco-friendly, but many drivers doubt that they can be real fun. Which is wrong, when it comes to the smart fortwo electric drive: it has a surprisingly powerful acceleration from a standing start. We wanted to make people rethink.

2. SOLUTION: A redesign of the popular video game PONG, featuring the smart fortwo electric drive. smart EBALL ist played by driving the car quickly back and forth. In other words: the cars turn into the controllers. And each driver can see for themselves the surprising acceleration and driving enjoyment.

3. RESULT: The strong visual of smart EBALL went around the world: countless visitors uploaded posts and videos, blogs took up the subject, it was being discussed on TV and in the press. Over 10 days at the IAA Frankfurt, the biggest motor show in the world, 520,000 spectators watched 3,000 EBALL games.

SMART EBALL GAME:

- A redesign of the popular video game PONG
- The cars are turned into controllers
- Creating a strong visual that went around the world
- Designed to make people rethink electric cars

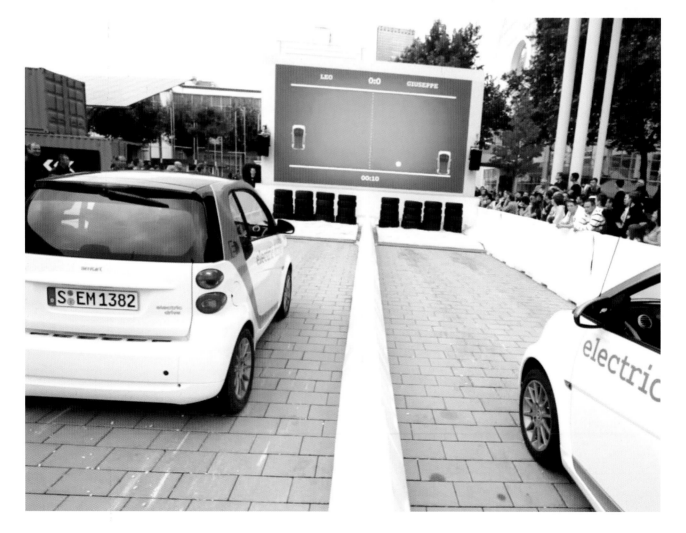

THE FIRST COMPUTER GAME, WHERE CARS ARE USED AS CONTROLLERS.

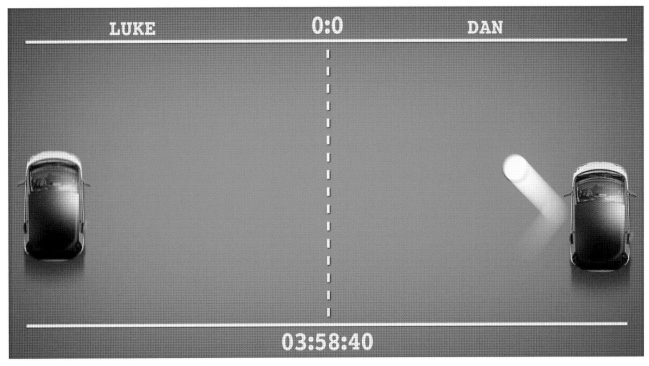

SMART EBALL
BBDO PROXIMITY BERLIN GMBH
Physical | Innovation

CHIEF CREATIVE OFFICER: Jan Harbeck,
David Mously, Wolfgang Schneider
CREATIVE DIRECTOR: Ton Hollander,
Jens Ringena
ART DIRECTOR: Daniel Schweinzer,
Sebastian Forsman, Tomas Tulinius
COPYWRITER: Lukas Liske, Fredric Antonsson
ANIMATOR: nhb studios Berlin GmbH, Berlin
HEAD OF TV: Steffen Gentis
PRODUCER: Silke Rochow, Julia Diehl,
Bernd Mueller, Ernst Fluegel, Michael Plfanz
PRODUCTION COMPANY:
Gahrens + Battermann GmbH,
Bergisch Gladbach, e.w.enture GmbH, Munich,
Pflanz Werbemittelproduktion GmbH, Berlin

VISUAL EFFECTS: nhb studios Berlin GmbH, Berlin
SOUND DESIGN: nhb ton GmbH, Hamburg
GROUP HEAD: Frank Haegele (BBDO Live),
Sandra Gesell (BBDO Live)
ACCOUNT DIRECTOR: Dirk Spakowski,
Sebastian Schlosser, Jan Hendrick Oelckers
CLIENT: Daimler AG
COUNTRY: Germany

LULLABIES
FORSMAN & BODENFORS
Website | Campaign Site

ART DIRECTOR: Adam Ulvegärde,
Andreas Malm
COPYWRITER: Elisabeth Christensson,
Fredrik Jansson
DESIGNER: Christoffer Persson
PHOTOGRAPHER: Carl Nilsson
DIRECTOR: RBG6
PRODUCTION COMPANY:
Christian Zubick (KokoKaka Entertainment)
MUSIC/COMPOSER: Music Super Circus
CLIENT: IKEA
COUNTRY: Sweden

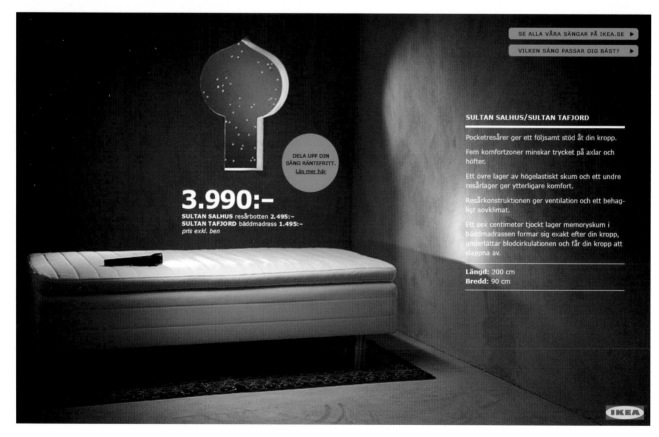

OBSESSED WITH SOUND
TRIBAL DDB AMSTERDAM
Website | Campaign Site

EXECUTIVE CREATIVE DIRECTOR: Chris Baylis
ART DIRECTOR: Bart Mol
COPYWRITER: Pol Hoenderboom
DESIGNER: Robbin Cenijn, Ian Bauer
DIRECTOR OF PHOTOGRAPHY:
Matias Boucard
DIRECTOR: Rob Chiu
EDITOR: Nikaj Gouwerok (VET)
PRODUCTION COMPANY: StinkDigital
SOUND DESIGN: Joep Beving,
Cris Kos (Massive Music)
MUSIC COMPOSER: Metropole Orchestra,
Berend Dubbe, Mark Pytlik
PROJECT MANAGER: Jeroen Jedeloo,
Richard Land, Christy Wassenaar
ACCOUNT DIRECTOR: Sandra Krstic
CLIENT: Philips
COUNTRY: Netherlands

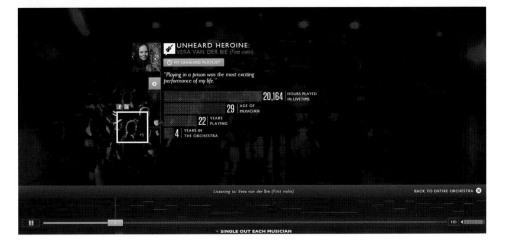

ROME
GOOGLE CREATIVE LAB
Website | Innovation

CREATIVE DIRECTOR: Chris Milk
ANIMATOR: Mirada
PRODUCTION COMPANY: @radical.media
PROGRAMMER: Mr.Doob, Google Data Arts Team
AGENCY: North Kingdom
CLIENT: Google
COUNTRY: United States

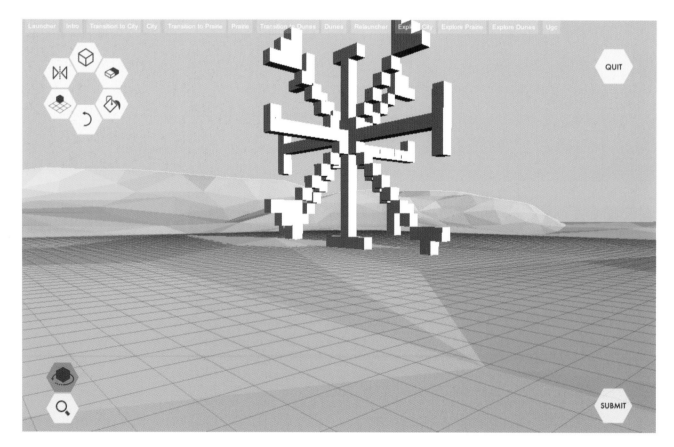

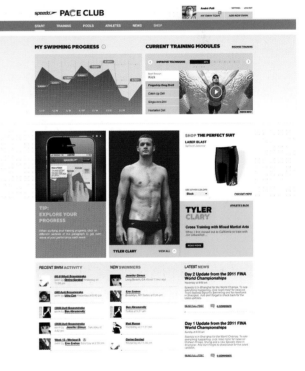

SPEEDO PACE CLUB
SYRUP
Social | Social Network Platform

EXECUTIVE CREATIVE DIRECTOR:
Jakob Daschek
CHIEF CREATIVE OFFICER: Jakob Daschek
CREATIVE DIRECTOR: Alex Lins,
Benjamin Abramowitz
COPYWRITER: Spencer LaVallee
DESIGNER: Andre Luiz Poli
PRODUCER: Joe Croson
ACCOUNT DIRECTOR: Nii Addo, Erin Endres
CLIENT: Speedo USA
COUNTRY: United States

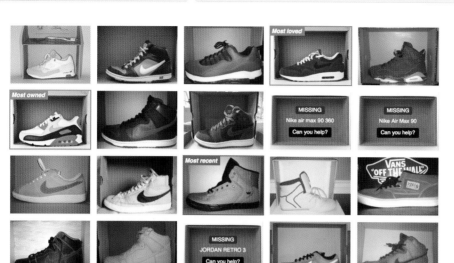

SNEAKERPEDIA
SAPIENTNITRO LONDON
Social | Social Network Platform

CHIEF CREATIVE OFFICER: Malcolm Poynton
INTERACTIVE DESIGNER: Robbie Davies,
Andy Haijitheodoulou, Jyotish Nair
INFORMATION ARCHITECT: Giles Perry,
Dean Wilson
CREATIVE TECHNOLOGY: Cat Le-Huy
INTERACTIVE DEVELOPER: Ben Dunkley,
Mick Horler, David Strugnell, Shaun Dunne
TECHNICAL DELIVERY MANAGER: Mike Smith
SOCIAL MEDIA STRATEGY:
Kate Eltringham, Charles Wells
PROJECT MANAGEMENT: David Mercado
PROGRAM MANAGEMENT:
Helen Curtis-Jenkins
GROUP ACCOUNT DIRECTOR: James Graham
ACCOUNT DIRECTOR: Kate Eltringham
CLIENT: Foot Locker Europe
COUNTRY: United Kingdom

DIG DEEPER
BBDO NEW YORK
Social | Online Game

EXECUTIVE CREATIVE DIRECTOR:
Greg Hahn, Mike Smith
CHIEF CREATIVE OFFICER: David Lubars
ART DIRECTOR: Marcel Yunes
COPYWRITER: Rick Williams
DIRECTOR OF PHOTOGRAPHY:
Christopher Soos
DIRECTOR: Tim Godsall
EDITOR: Geoff Hounsell
EXECUTIVE PRODUCER: Holly Vega
PRODUCER: Colleen O'Donnell
LINE PRODUCER: Mala Vasan
PRODUCTION COMPANY: Biscuit
Filmworks, B-Reel
SOUND DESIGN: Henryboy
CLIENT: HBO/True Blood
COUNTRY: United States

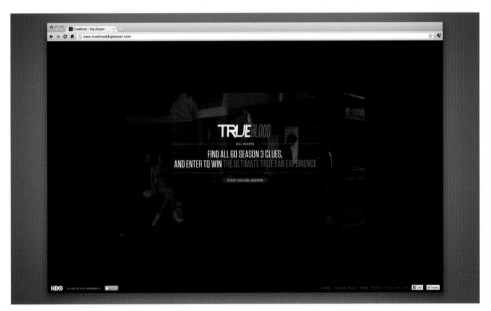

HEINEKEN STAR PLAYER
AKQA
Social | Online Game

CHAIRMAN: Ajaz Ahmed
EXECUTIVE CREATIVE DIRECTOR: Nick Bailey
CHIEF CREATIVE OFFICER: James Hilton
CREATIVE DIRECTOR: Miles Unwin
ASSOCIATE CREATIVE DIRECTOR:
Kevin Russell
ART DIRECTOR: Jamen Percy
SENIOR COPYWRITER: Tessa Hawson
PROJECT DIRECTOR: Hanna Gray
PROJECT MANAGER: Carolyn Mangan
GROUP ACCOUNT DIRECTOR: James Scott
CLIENT: Heineken
COUNTRY: United Kingdom

THE MUSEUM OF ME
PROJECTOR INC.
Social | Social Network Innovation

CREATIVE DIRECTOR:
Koichiro Tanaka, Seiichi Saito
DESIGN DIRECTOR: Toru Hayai
ART DIRECTOR: Masanori Sakamoto
COPYWRITER: Lilia Silva
DESIGNER: Hiroshi Takeyama, Takashi Yasuno,
Yuuki Nemoto, Mitsuhiro Azuma
DIRECTOR: Eiji Tanigawa
PRODUCER: Satoshi Takahashi

PRODUCTION COMPANY: TAIYO KIKAKU
co., ltd., Rhizomatiks co., ltd., DELTRO INC.,
MountPosition Inc.
MUSIC/COMPOSER: Takagi Masakatsu
PROGRAMMER: Ken Murayama,
Hajime Sasaki, Hirohisa Mitsuishi
PROJECT MANAGER: Shimpei Oshima
CLIENT: Intel
COUNTRY: Japan

DREAM RECOMMENDER
TWOFIFTEENMCCANN
Online Content | Non-Broadcast Media

EXECUTIVE CREATIVE DIRECTOR:
Scott Duchon, John Patroulis
CREATIVE DIRECTOR:
Paul Caiozzo, Nathan Frank,
Jason Jones (Lifelong Friendship Society)
INTERACTIVE CREATIVE DIRECTOR:
Magnus Oliv
ART DIRECTOR: Paul Caiozzo, Nathan Frank,
Phillip Fivel Nessen
COPYWRITER: Paul Caiozzo, Nathan Frank
PRODUCTION DESIGNER: Peter Benson
ILLUSTRATOR: Phillip Fivel Nessen
DIRECTOR OF PHOTOGRAPHY:
Rogier Stoffers (Tool of North America),
Sean Kirby (Lifelong Friendship Society)
ANIMATOR: Sid Seed, Dan Short, Jay Kim,
Danny Kamhaji (Lifelong Friendship Society),
Molly Wengert (We Are Licious)
DIRECTOR:
Geordie Stephens (Tool of North America),
Jason Jones (Lifelong Friendship Society)
EDITOR: Christjan Jordan (Arcade Edit),
Will Hasell
AGENCY DIRECTOR OF INTEGRATED
PRODUCTION: Tom Wright
HEAD OF PRODUCTION:
Amy DeLossa (Tool of North America)
EXECUTIVE PRODUCER:
Matt Bonin (Tool of North America), Brain Latt,
Dustin Callif (Lifelong Friendship Society),
Dan Sormani (Arcade Edit), Deanne Mehling
AGENCY PRODUCER: Mandie Bowe,
Joyce Chen, Ali Reed (Arcade Edit)
LINE PRODUCER:
Mark Fetterman (Tool of North America),
Kim Koby (Lifelong Friendship Society)
PRODUCTION COMPANY:
Tool of North America,
Lifelong Friendship Society
DIGITAL PRODUCTION COMPANY:
We Are Licious
VISUAL EFFECTS: Lifelong Friendship Society
MUSIC/COMPOSER: Human
ACCOUNT SUPERVISOR: Melissa Hill
CLIENT: Help Remedies
COUNTRY: United States

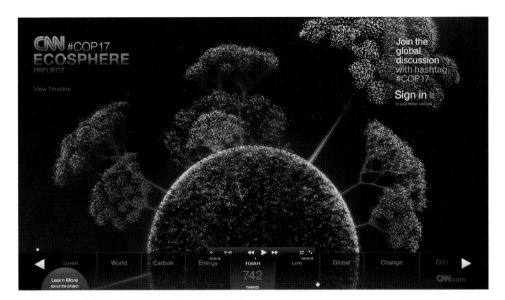

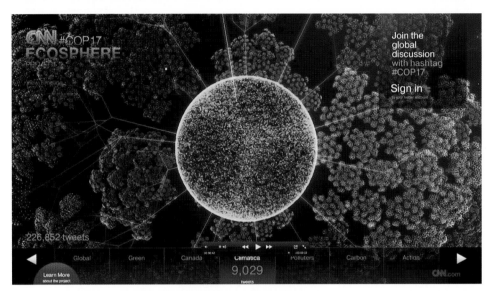

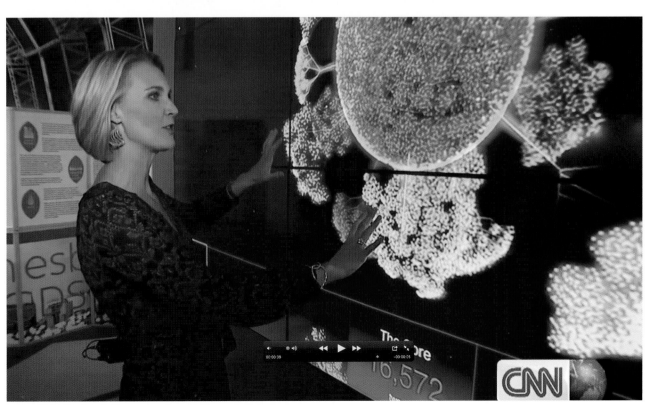

THE CNN ECOSPHERE
HEIMAT
Online Content | Data Visualization

EXECUTIVE CREATIVE DIRECTOR:
Guido Heffels
CHIEF CREATIVE OFFICER: Myles Lord,
Martien Delfgaauw
DESIGN DIRECTOR: Jue Alt
SENIOR ART DIRECTOR: Frank Hose,
Luc Schurgers
COPYWRITER: Ramin Schmiedekampf
DIRECTOR: Minivegas/Amsterdam
EDITOR: Alexander Suchy
EXECUTIVE PRODUCER: James Briton,
Mark Pytlik, Nils Schwemer
PRODUCTION COMPANY: StinkDigital
VISUAL EFFECTS: StinkDigital
PROGRAMMER: Minivegas
PROJECT MANAGER: Jessica Valin
CLIENT: CNN International
COUNTRY: Germany

INTEGRATED

INTERACTIVE
Online Content | Online Content Innovation

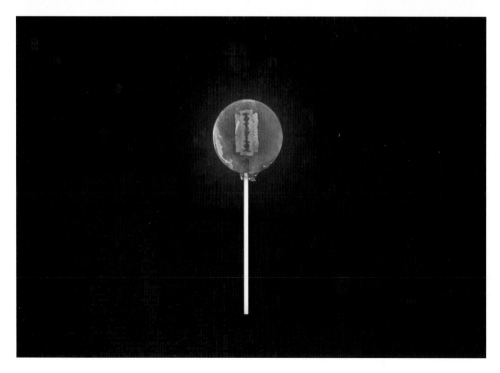

TAKE THIS LOLLIPOP
TOOL
Online Content | Innovation

DIRECTOR: Jason Zada
EXECUTIVE PRODUCER: Brian Latt,
Oliver Fuselier, Dustin Callif
PRODUCTION COMPANY: Tool
MUSIC/COMPOSER: Future Perfect
PROGRAMMER: Jason Nickel
AGENCY: Little Monster
CLIENT: Little Monster
COUNTRY: United States

KEY TO VIANO
LUKAS LINDEMANN ROSINSKI GMBH
Physical | Innovation

EXECUTIVE CREATIVE DIRECTOR:
Arno Lindemann, Bernhard Lukas
CREATIVE DIRECTOR: Markus Kremer,
Thomas Heyen
ART DIRECTOR: Moritz Frehse
COPYWRITER: Teja Fischer, Tobias Schroeder
DIRECTOR: Tibor Glage
PRODUCER: Henrike Boege, Martin Schoen
PRODUCTION COMPANY: Markenfilm Crossing
VISUAL EFFECTS: Alexander Schillinsky,
Pablo Bach (Liga_01 Hamburg)
PROGRAMMER: Carsten Schwiering,
Tim Isenheim
PUBLISHER: Askan Lerche, Nadja Vogel,
Harald Mertens
PROJECT MANAGER: Jascha Oevermann,
Gero Quast
CLIENT: Mercedes Benz Vans
COUNTRY: Germany

URBAN TOUR
BBH LONDON
Website | Campaign Site

CREATIVE DIRECTOR: Dominic Oldman
ART DIRECTOR: Dominic Oldman
COPYWRITER: David Kolbusz
INTERACTIVE DESIGN: Eric Chia
DIRECTOR: Sebastian Strasser
PRODUCER: Olivia Chalk
PRODUCTION COMPANY: Pulse Films,
Stink TV, StinkDigital
ACCOUNT DIRECTOR: Ngaio Pardon,
Liz Harper
CLIENT: Asos.com
COUNTRY: United Kingdom

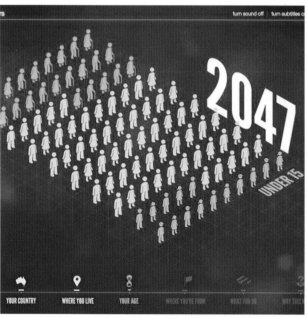

SPOTLIGHT
LEO BURNETT SYDNEY
Website | Campaign Site

CHIEF CREATIVE OFFICER: Andy DiLallo
CREATIVE DIRECTOR: Kieran Ots
ART DIRECTOR: Kieran Ots, Sharon Edmonton
COPYWRITER: Kieran Ots, Misha McDonald
DESIGNER: Dave Mugford, Eddy Milfort,
Janifer Wong
ILLUSTRATOR: John-Henry Pajak
PRODUCER: Lester Martinez, Jennifer Borres
MUSIC/COMPOSER: Chris Bradstreet
PROGRAMMER: Keong Seet, William Parry,
Kevin Brown
CLIENT: Australian Bureau of Statistics
COUNTRY: Australia

DOVE NFL
GRUPOW
Online Content | Banners

CLIENT: Unilever, Dove Men Care
COUNTRY: Mexico

BILLBOARD POWERED BY ORANGES
DDB PARIS
Online Content | Original Web Commercials

CHAIRMAN: Jean-Luc Bravi,
Matthieu de Lesseux
EXECUTIVE CREATIVE DIRECTOR:
Alexandre Hervè
CREATIVE DIRECTOR: Alexander Kalchev,
Siavosh Zabeti
DESIGN DIRECTOR: Alex Marden (Artem UK)
ART DIRECTOR: Alexander Kalchev,
Siavosh Zabeti
COPYWRITER: Alexander Kalchev,
Siavosh Zabeti
DIRECTOR: Johnny Hardstaff

EDITOR: Ed Cheesman
EXECUTIVE PRODUCER: Piero Frescobaldi
PRODUCER: Michelle Craig
PRODUCTION COMPANY: Unit 9
SOUND DESIGN: THE
PHOTO EDITOR: Clemens Ascher
ACCOUNT DIRECTOR: Julie Régis,
Edouard Teixeira
ART BUYER: Guillaume Cossou,
Florence Gabet
CLIENT: Tropicana
COUNTRY: France

NIKE SPARQ
R/GA
Mobile | Mobile Experience Marketing

CHAIRMAN: Bob Greenberg
CHIEF CREATIVE OFFICER: Nick Law
CREATIVE DIRECTOR: Albert Patton,
Sammi Needham
ART DIRECTOR: Rasmus Wangelin
COPYWRITER: Devin Heatley
DESIGNER: Mike Lee
EDITOR: Chris Shimojima
HEAD OF PRODUCTION: Vin Farrell
PRODUCER: Beam Seilaudom, Guy Helson,
Jon Jones, Nick Parisi, Lexi Steigelman
PROGRAMMER: Jack Bishop, Jane Yang,
Ryan Wang, Vincent Dibartolo, Will Creedle
CLIENT: Nike Football
COUNTRY: United States

INTEGRATED

ADIDAS X GIANTS: DIGITAL TRYOUT
TBWA\HAKUHODO
Mobile | Mobile Experience Marketing

EXECUTIVE CREATIVE DIRECTOR:
Kazoo Sato
CREATIVE DIRECTOR: Hideyuki Tanaka
ART DIRECTOR: Haruhito Nisawadaira,
Keisuke Shimizu
COPYWRITER: Masaharu Kumagai
DIRECTOR: Yasuhiko Shimizu
PRODUCER: Kentaro Kinoshita (TYO Inc.)
PRODUCTION COMPANY: TYO Inc.
CLIENT: adidas Japan K.K.
COUNTRY: Japan

Interactive
Merits

XC TRAVELS
FORSMAN & BODENFORS
Website | Campaign Site

ART DIRECTOR: Staffan Lamm, Andreas Malm
COPYWRITER: Fredrik Jansson
DESIGNER: Mikko Timonen
PRODUCTION COMPANY:
North Kingdom, Acne, Thomson Interactive
MUSIC/COMPOSER: Music Super Service
ACCOUNT DIRECTOR: Anders Bothen
ADVERTISER'S SUPERVISOR: Bengt Junemo
CLIENT: Volvo Cars Sweden
COUNTRY: Sweden

GOTHENBURG TRAM SEIGHTSEEING
FORSMAN & BODENFORS
Mobile | Mobile Experience Marketing

ART DIRECTOR: Lars Jansson,
Staffan Forsman
COPYWRITER: Anders Hegerfors
DESIGNER: Staffan Håkansson
PRODUCTION COMPANY: Mad In Sweden
ACCOUNT DIRECTOR: Greger Andersson
ADVERTISER'S SUPERVISOR:
Suzanne Erikson
CLIENT: Västtrafik
COUNTRY: Sweden

D-DAY TO VICTORY INTERACTIVE
SECRET LOCATION
Website

CREATIVE DIRECTOR: Pietro Gagliano
ART DIRECTOR: Steve Miller, Ryan Cherewaty
COPYWRITER: Jonathan Pottins
DESIGNER: Kai Salminen
ILLUSTRATOR: Jordan Nieuwland
ANIMATOR: Steve Miller, Ryan Cherewaty
PROGRAMMER: Ryan Andal, Michael Phan,
Gino Fazari
EDITOR: Kelly Manchester
EXECUTIVE PRODUCER: James Milward
PRODUCER: Noora Abu Eitah
VISUAL EFFECTS: Anthony Murray
SOUND DESIGN: Lodewijk Vos
MUSIC/COMPOSER: Alex Khaskin
CLIENT: Shaw Media
COUNTRY: Canada

THE VIRTUAL FOOTWEAR WALL
START JUDGEGILL
Physical | Innovation

CLIENT: adidas
COUNTRY: United Kingdom

Advertising is tougher than ever.

Advertising Jury

Advertising

This show has soul. Maybe owing to its 91-year heritage or the fact that pretty much every luminary from the worlds of design and advertising have at one time been part of it, but the ADC and this show, in particular, has something about it that many lack: It uniquely slants the attention of judges to the spirit of the artist who, although willingly serving commerce, aspires to bring a little grace and surprise to advertising. So, when this hugely accomplished group of international judges started, we discussed how our objective would be of course to uphold the high standards of the ADC, but also that the awarded work should provoke some questions in the progressive spirit of the ADC. While it is true that many of our selections were harbingers for the success of work in shows to come, thankfully there were some oddballs and gems that may have otherwise gone overlooked. And that is a great expression of the unique spirit of the ADC: Rewarding experimentation as well as professional excellence. After all, a great ADC show, and the work awarded in it, should not only be a definitive statement of excellence, but also create some provocative questions for folks to address and answer over time.

John Boiler
Advertising Jury Chair

Advertising Jury

John Boiler
72andSunny
United States

Vanessa Fortier
The Martin Agency
United States

Jack Mariucci
M&M Creative Group,
School of Visual Arts
United States

Hunter Fine
BBDO New York
United States

Kobi Barki
Draftfcb+
Shimoni Finkelstein Barki
Israel

Frank Hahn
72andSunny
United States

Haydn Morris
mcgarrybowen
United States

Akira Kagami
Dentsu
Japan

Andy Blood
WHYBIN\TBWA\Tequila
New Zealand

Keith Ho
The Association of
Accredited Advertising
Agencies of Hong Kong
Hong Kong

Martin Ringqvist
Forsman & Bodenfors
Sweden

Ari Weiss
BBH New York
United States

Paul Cohen
DDB Chicago
United States

Colin Jeffrey
David&Goliath
United States

Michael Schachtner
BBH New York
United States

Mark Wenneker
Mullen
United States

Susan Credle
Leo Burnett Chicago
United States

Joe Johnson
Publicis New York
United States

Darren Spiller
Fallon Worldwide
United States

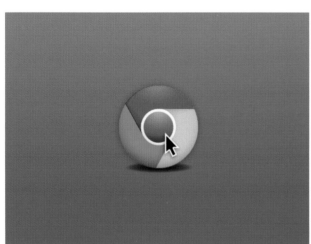

the web is what you make of it

THE WEB IS WHAT YOU MAKE OF IT
BBH NEW YORK &
GOOGLE CREATIVE LAB
TV/Film | Television Commercial

CLIENT: Google
COUNTRY: United States

Google Chrome: Dear Sophie for
ADVERTISING Broadcast Craft | Editing

itgetsbetterproject 12 videos ⌄ Subscribe

THE BEAR
BETC
TV/Film | Television Commercial

CHIEF CREATIVE OFFICER: Stéphane Xiberras
ART DIRECTOR: Eric Astorgue
COPYWRITER: Jean-Christophe Royer
DIRECTOR OF PHOTOGRAPHY:
Joost Van Gelder
DIRECTOR: Matthijs van Heijningen
EDITOR: Jono Griffiths
PRODUCER: Isabelle Menard, David Green
PRODUCTION COMPANY: Soixante Quinze
(Yuki Suga)
VISUAL EFFECTS: Mikros
SOUND DESIGN: Gum, Éric Cervera
(near deaf experience)
ACCOUNT DIRECTOR: Raphael de Andreis
CLIENT: CANAL+
COUNTRY: France

ADVERTISING | TV/Film | Cinema Commercial
ADVERTISING | Broadcast Craft | Direction

ADVERTISING | Broadcast Craft | Art Direction
ADVERTISING | Broadcast Craft | Copywriting

PATHOLOGICAL LIAR
Y&R NEW YORK
Broadcast Craft | Copywriting

EXECUTIVE CREATIVE DIRECTOR:
Kerry Keenan, Ian Reichenthal, Scott Vitrone
CREATIVE DIRECTOR: Guillermo Vega,
Graham Lang, Steve Whittier
ART DIRECTOR: Michael Schachtner
COPYWRITER: Julia Neumann
DIRECTOR OF PHOTOGRAPHY:
Antonio Calvache
DIRECTOR: David Shane
EDITOR: Jason MacDonald (Number Six)
HEAD OF PRODUCTION: Lora Schulson,
Nathy Aviram
EXECUTIVE PRODUCER: Ralph Laucella
PRODUCER: Mara Milicevic, Jona Goodman
PRODUCTION COMPANY: O Positive Films
SOUND DESIGN: Sound Lounge, New York
CLIENT: Land Rover
COUNTRY: United States

HEAVEN AND HELL
JWT SHANGHAI
Press Craft | Art Direction

EXECUTIVE CREATIVE DIRECTOR:
SheungYan Lo, Yang Yeo, Elvis Chau
CREATIVE DIRECTOR: Hattie Cheng,
Rojana Chuasakul
SENIOR ART DIRECTOR: Rojana Chuasakul,
Surachai Puthikulangkur
ART DIRECTOR: Haoxi Lv, Danny Li
COPYWRITER: Marc Wang
ILLUSTRATOR: Surachai Puthikulangkura,
SupachaiU-Rairat

ANIMATOR: Illusion Co. Ltd.
LINE PRODUCER: Anotai Panmongkol,
Somsak Pairew
PRODUCTION COMPANY: Illusion Co. Ltd.
ACCOUNT DIRECTOR: Tom Doctoroff, Sophia
Ng, Lily Zheng, Michelle Xiao, Maggie Zhou
CLIENT: Samsonite
COUNTRY: China

THE INVISIBLE DRIVE
JUNG VON MATT AG
Ambient/Environmental | Stunts/Guerrilla

EXECUTIVE CREATIVE OFFICER: Armin Jochum
CHIEF CREATIVE OFFICER: Thimoteus Wagner,
Fabian Frese, Götz Ulmer
CREATIVE DIRECTOR: Michael Ohanian,
Jonas Keller, Martin Strutz
ART DIRECTOR: Jonas Keller, Andreas Wagner
COPYWRITER: Michael Ohanian
DESIGNER: Daniel Soares
DIRECTOR OF PHOTOGRAPHY: Jakob Süß
DIRECTOR: Daniel Schmidt
EDITOR: Daniel Schmidt
PRODUCER: Martin Schön
PRODUCTION COMPANY:
Markenfilm-Crossing GmbH
RETOUCHER: Tina Rentzsch
PROGRAMMER: Christopher Schultz,
Bettina Ackermann
PROJECT MANAGER: Ann-Kathrin Geertz,
Kete Stodtmeister, Nelli Walker
ACCOUNT DIRECTOR: Sven Dörrenbächer,
Sonja Stockmann
CLIENT: Daimler AG
COUNTRY: Germany

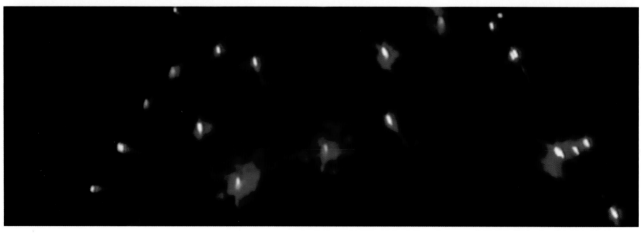

SI LA NAVIDAD PUDO LLEGAR HASTA LA SELVA,
USTED TAMBIÉN PUEDE LLEGAR HASTA SU CASA.

DESMOVILÍCESE. EN NAVIDAD TODO ES POSIBLE.

IF CHRISTMAS CAN COME TO THE JUNGLE, YOU CAN COME HOME.

DESIGNISM

DAY 1
PLANNING:

2 BLACK HAWK
HELICOPTERS

LED
CHRISTMAS LIGHTS

We hope that bringing this Christmas message to the guerrilla,

HALFTIME AMERICA
WIEDEN+KENNEDY
TV/Film | Television Commercial

EXECUTIVE CREATIVE DIRECTOR:
Susan Hoffman, Mark Fitzloff
CHIEF CREATIVE OFFICER: Dan Wieden
CREATIVE DIRECTOR: Aaron Allen, Joe Staples,
Michael Tabtabai
ART DIRECTOR: Jimm Lasser
COPYWRITER: Kevin Jones, Smith Henderson,
Matthew Dickman
DIRECTOR OF PHOTOGRAPHY: Eric Treml
DIRECTOR: David Gordon Green
EDITOR: Tommy Harden
AGENCY EXECUTIVE PRODUCER:
Ben Grylewicz
EXECUTIVE PRODUCER: Corey Bartha,
Allison Amon, Lisa Mehling,
Patrick McGoldrick (Chelsea)
PRODUCER: Bob Wendt
LINE PRODUCER: Melinda Nugent
PRODUCTION COMPANY: Chelsea
VISUAL EFFECTS: Method Studios
SOUND DESIGN: Revolver Studios
MUSIC/COMPOSER: Alison Ables
PROJECT MANAGER: Tamar Berk
ACCOUNT DIRECTOR: Thomas Harvey,
Lani Reichenbach, David Newsome
CLIENT: Chrysler Group LLC
COUNTRY: United States

LG THIEF
Y&R AMSTERDAM
TV/Film | Non-Broadcast Commercial

CREATIVE DIRECTOR: Lionell Schuring,
Sheldon Bont
ART DIRECTOR: Theo Korf, Nick Plomp
COPYWRITER: Andrew Maaldrink
DIRECTOR: Hans Knaapen
EDITOR: Electric Zoo
PRODUCER: Sandra Verbaas,
Maarten van Hemmen
LINE PRODUCER: Chantal Gulpers,
Denise Willigers
PRODUCTION COMPANY: Electric Zoo
VISUAL EFFECTS: Postoffice Amsterdam
SOUND DESIGN: Postoffice Amsterdam
CLIENT: LG Electronics Benelux
COUNTRY: Netherlands

BALLOONS
LODUCCA
Broadcast Craft | Art Direction

CREATIVE DIRECTOR: Guga Ketzer,
Cassio Moron, Pedro Guerra, Marco Monteiro
ART DIRECTOR: Guga Ketzer, Andre Faria,
Dulcidio Caldeira
COPYWRITER: Guga Ketzer, Andre Faria,
Dulcidio Caldeira
ILLUSTRATOR: Daniel Semanas
DIRECTOR OF PHOTOGRAPHY:
Alexandre Ermel
ANIMATOR: Daniel Semanas
DIRECTOR: Dulcidio Caldeira
EXECUTIVE PRODUCER: Egisto Betti,
Ana Luisa Andre, Sid Fernandes
PRODUCER: Karina Vadasz
PRODUCTION COMPANY: Paranoid BR
SOUND DESIGN: Raw Produtora de Audio
MUSIC: William Tell Overture
COMPOSER: Gioachino Rossini
ACCOUNT DIRECTOR: Carmen Assumpção,
Sabrina Spinelli
CLIENT: MTV Brasil
COUNTRY: Brazil

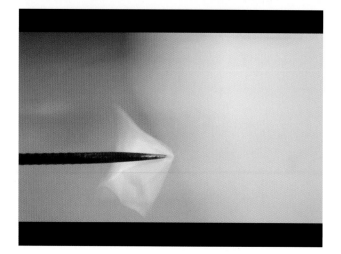

PARALLELS
STRAWBERRY FROG
Broadcast Craft | Art Direction

CHIEF CREATIVE OFFICER: Kevin McKeon
CREATIVE DIRECTOR: Josh Greenspan,
Jason Koxvold
COPYWRITER: Josh Greenspan, Todd Beeby
MANAGING DIRECTOR: Sophie Kelly
DIRECTOR: Dante Ariola
EDITOR: Adam Pertofsky
EXECUTIVE PRODUCER: David Zander,
Jeff Scruton
PRODUCER: Sherri Levy
LINE PRODUCER: Natalie Hill
PRODUCTION COMPANY: MJZ
MUSIC: Human
ACCOUNT DIRECTOR: Sherri Chambers
EDITING COMPANY: Rock Paper Scissors
EFX: The Mill
SPECIAL MAKEUP EFFECTS: Legacy Effects
SPECIAL MAKEUP EFFECTS SUPERVISOR:
J. Alan Scott
SPECIAL MAKEUP EFFECTS ARTISTS:
Scott Stoddard, Mike Smithson, Chris Gallaher
SPECIAL WIGS AND HAIRPIECES:
Aimee Macabeo
CUSTOM TATTOOS:
Jim Charmatz, Corey Castallano
AGENCY: MJZ
CLIENT: Jim Beam
COUNTRY: United States

ADVERTISING | Broadcast Craft | Direction

ADVERTISING | Broadcast Craft | Cinematography

TOSHIBA LED BULB - 10 YEAR CALENDAR

CHALLENGE
To introduce Toshiba's new LED bulb that lasts over 10 years.

IDEA
A 10-year calendar to demonstrate exactly how long the LED bulb lasts. Each day is a silhouette from the same room lighted by a LED bulb. We posted this huge poster on a gigantic wall so that the passersby can see inside each room and follow the story.

STORY
A young man lives alone at first. One day he starts dating a girl and they fall in love. They decide to get married and soon they are blessed with a beautiful baby boy. Dad, mom and the boy enjoy events like Christmas, Halloween, birthdays and so on. Eventually the baby boy becomes a big brother with the birth of his sister. In the end, the happy family grows to five but one thing hasn't changed for all of the ten years: the LED bulb.

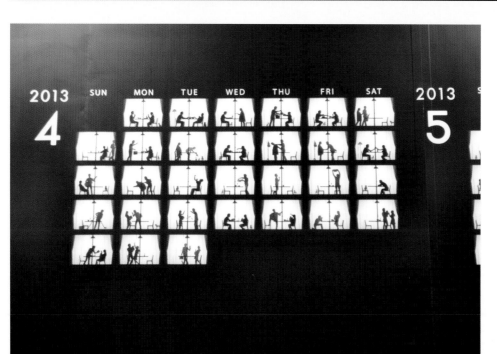

WITH 10 YEARS OF LIFE
DENTSU INC.
Poster or Billboard | Outdoor/Billboard

CHAIRMAN: Kenichirou Matsumoto (Toshiba)
VICE CHAIRMAN:Shunji Suzuki (Toshiba),
Ako Hatano (Toshiba)
CHIEF CREATIVE OFFICER: Makoto Takeuchi
CREATIVE DIRECTOR: Masumi Nakazawa
ART DIRECTOR: Tsubasa Adachi
COPYWRITER: Jumpei Iwata, Yuichi Kitada,
Sayaka Arimoto
DESIGNER: Takahiro Shibata, Chihiro Shiraisi,
Kensaku Hidaka
PHOTOGRAPHER: Shingo Fujimoto
AGENCY PRODUCER: Akiko Seino
PHOTO PRODUCER: Kazuhiro Hoshimoto
RETOUCHER: Hiroyuki Nakagawa
CLIENT: Toshiba Corporation
COUNTRY: Japan

The names promotion
50% on items with the same name as you.

Challenge

Every year, the big furniture retail chains inundate consumers with advertising for their new range. We looked for a new way of making consumers take a much closer look at Micasa furniture and accessories.

WILLIAM CLARA GIULIA JOE HENRY AURELIA JASMIN VIRGINIA

Idea

Many of the items in the Micasa range have the same names as people. We used this to launch a very special kind of sales promotion. Consumers who can find an article with the same name as themselves get it for half price.

TV-Spots

Billboards

"If your name is Jasmin, please call me. I want this furniture."

Results

More orders for the catalogue in a month than in the entire year before.
The website received twice as many klicks as usual.
And of course, many happy customers!

  micasa.ch ×2

Marlene Alice Sandra

NAMES-PROMOTION
SPILLMANN/FELSER/LEO BURNETT
Collateral | Promotional

CREATIVE DIRECTOR: Martin Spillmann,
Peter Broennimann
ART DIRECTOR: Pablo Schencke,
Christian Bobst
COPYWRITER: Johannes Raggio
CLIENT: Micasa
COUNTRY: Switzerland

OCCUPY GEORGE
OCCUPY GEORGE
Ambient/Environmental | Small Scale

CREATIVE DIRECTOR: Andy Dao, Ivan Cash
PROGRAMMER: Scott Blew
CLIENT: Occupy George
COUNTRY: United States

RIVALRY
HUNGRY MAN
TV/Film | Television Commercial

CREATIVE DIRECTOR: The Brooklyn Brothers
COPYWRITER: Charlie Grandy, Mike Schur
DIRECTOR OF PHOTOGRAPHY:
Scott Henriksen
DIRECTOR: Bryan Buckley
EXECUTIVE PRODUCER: Kevin Byrne
PRODUCER: Mino Janjoura
PRODUCTION COMPANY: Hungry Man
AGENCY: The Brooklyn Brothers
CLIENT: New Era
COUNTRY: United States

CAB JAM
MULLEN
TV/Film | Television Commercial

EXECUTIVE CREATIVE DIRECTOR:
Mark Wenneker
CHIEF CREATIVE OFFICER: Mark Wenneker
CREATIVE DIRECTOR: Tim Vaccarino,
Jamie Ferreira, Dave Weist
SENIOR ART DIRECTOR: Tim Vaccarino,
Jamie Ferreira
COPYWRITER: Dave Weist
HEAD OF PRODUCTION: Liza Near
EXECUTIVE PRODUCER: Zeke Bowman
PRODUCTION COMPANY: Smuggler
VISUAL EFFECTS: Brickyard VFX
SOUND DESIGN: Soundtrack Studios
ACCOUNT DIRECTOR: Michael Craig
CLIENT: JetBlue
COUNTRY: United States

ESPN BRAND "SHAKE ON IT"
WIEDEN+KENNEDY NEW YORK
TV/Film | Television Commercial

EXECUTIVE CREATIVE DIRECTOR:
Ian Reichenthal, Scott Vitrone
CREATIVE DIRECTOR: Stuart Jennings,
Brandon Henderson
ART DIRECTOR: Cyrus Coulter
COPYWRITER: Dave Canning
DIRECTOR OF PHOTOGRAPHY: Linus Sandgren
DIRECTOR: Aaron Stoller
EDITOR: Ian Mackenzie (Mackenzie Cutler)
EDITORIAL COMPANY: Mackenize Cutler
HEAD OF CONTENT PRODUCTION: Gary Krieg
EXECUTIVE PRODUCER: Holly Vega (Biscuit),
Jill Silberstein (Sound Lounge)
PRODUCER: Cheryl Warbrook
LINE PRODUCER: Mala Vasan

POST PRODUCER: Sasha Hirschfeld
PRODUCTION COMPANY: Biscuit
VISUAL EFFECTS COMPANY: The Mill
VISUAL EFFECTS PRODUCER:
Charlotte Arnold (The Mill)
MUSIC & SOUND COMPANY: Pulse Music
MUSIC PRODUCER: Dan Kuby (Pulse Music)
MIX COMPANY: Sound Lounge
MIXER: Rob Sayers (Sound Lounge)
ACCOUNT TEAM: Brandon Pracht,
Casey Bernard, Brian d'Entremont,
Mark Williams
CLIENT: ESPN
COUNTRY: United States

SMUTLEY
GOODBY, SILVERSTEIN & PARTNERS
TV/Film | Television Small Budget

EXECUTIVE CREATIVE DIRECTOR:
Erik Vervroegen
SENIOR ART DIRECTOR: Andre Massis
COPYWRITER: Eric Boyd
DESIGNER: Johan Idesjö
DIRECTOR: Niklas Rissle, Kevin Grady
EXECUTIVE PRODUCER: Josh Thorne
PRODUCER: Jon Drawbaugh

LINE PRODUCER: Manuela Cripps
PRODUCTION COMPANY:
againstallodds, Stockholm
MUSIC/COMPOSER: Joan Jett
ACCOUNT DIRECTOR: Francois Grouiller
CLIENT: AIDES
COUNTRY: United States

THE DATE
WIEDEN+KENNEDY AMSTERDAM
Broadcast Craft | Art Direction

EXECUTIVE CREATIVE DIRECTOR:
Mark Bernath, Eric Queenoy
CREATIVE DIRECTOR: Mark Bernath,
Eric Queenoy
ART DIRECTOR: Alvaro Sotomayor
COPYWRITER: Roger Hoard
DIRECTOR OF PHOTOGRAPHY:
Mattias Montero
DIRECTOR: Fredrik Bond
EDITOR: Tim Thornton-Allan
HEAD OF PRODUCTION: Erik Verheijen
EXECUTIVE PRODUCER:
Helen Kenny (Sonny London)

PRODUCER: Tony Stearns, Niko Koot (AP)
PRODUCTION COMPANY: Sonny London
SOUND DESIGN: Raja Sehgal
MUSIC/COMPOSER: Mohammed Rafi,
Joan Pehechann Ho
PROJECT MANANGER: Sharon Kwiatkowski
ACCOUNT DIRECTOR: Clay Mills,
Jasmina Krnjetin
CLIENT: Heineken
COUNTRY: Netherlands

THE RECORDED CONTENTS
TBWA\ISTANBUL
Press | Newspaper Consumer Advertisement

EXECUTIVE CREATIVE DIRECTOR:
Ilkay Gurpinar
CREATIVE DIRECTOR: Emre Kaplan
ART DIRECTOR: Burak Kunduracioglu,
Ozlem Hanoglu

COPYWRITER: Ali Sener
ILLUSTRATOR: Omur Kokes,
Haluk Demirel, Anima
CLIENT: BEKO
COUNTRY: Turkey

MADE OF MORE
ABBOTT MEAD VICKERS BBDO
Broadcast Craft | Cinematography

EXECUTIVE CREATIVE DIRECTOR:
Paul Brazier
CREATIVE DIRECTOR: Paul Brazier
ART DIRECTOR: Paul Brazier
COPYWRITER: Paul Brazier
DIRECTOR: Tom Hooper

EDITOR: Paul Watts, Bruce Townsend
EXECUTIVE PRODUCER: Yvonne Chalkley
PRODUCER: Molly Pope
PRODUCTION COMPANY: INFINITY
CLIENT: Guinness
COUNTRY: United Kingdom

LUCK IS AN ATTITUDE
GORGEOUS
Broadcast Craft | Direction

CREATIVE DIRECTOR:
Fred Raillard. Farid Mokart
DIRECTOR OF PHOTOGRAPHY:
Damien Morisot
DIRECTOR: Peter Thwaites
EDITOR: Bill Smedley
PRODUCER: Anna Hashmi
PRODUCTION COMPANY: Gorgeous
VISUAL EFFECTS: The Mill
AGENCY: Fred & Farid Paris
CLIENT: Bacardi
COUNTRY: United Kingdom

PUB PAINTINGS
TBWA\CHIAT\DAY, NEW YORK
Poster or Billboard | Point-of-Purchase

CHAIRMAN: Mark Figliulo
CHIEF CREATIVE OFFICER: Mark Figliulo
CREATIVE DIRECTOR: Jonathan Mackler,
Alisa Sengel Wixom, Kris Wixom
ART DIRECTOR: Anthony DeCarolis,
Kevin Kaminishi, John Clement
COPYWRITER: Alisa Sengel Wixom,
Erik Fahrenkopf, Dan Giachetti, Aaron Stern,
Danny Gonzalez, David Suarez
ILLUSTRATOR: Steven J. Levin,
Domenick D'Andrea, Daniel Graves

HEAD OF PRODUCTION: Robert Valdes
PRODUCER: Katherine D'Addario,
John LaFaso
RETOUCHER: Erwin Brown, Daniel Finn,
Nancy Shaw, Randy Hiken
PROJECT MANAGER: Mimma Aliberti
ACCOUNT DIRECTOR: Lyndsey Corona
ART BUYER: Julia Menassa, Sydney Arkin,
Katie Johnson
CLIENT: Jameson
COUNTRY: United States

INTERRUPTIONS, MATCH
Y&R Argentina
Press | Newspaper Consumer Advertisement

EXECUTIVE CREATIVE DIRECTOR:
Martin Mercado
CREATIVE DIRECTOR: Diego Tuya, Dario Rial,
Martin Goldberg, Daniel Oliveira
ART DIRECTOR: Gonzalo Fernandez
COPYWRITER: Juan Ignacio Galardi
PHOTOGRAPHER: El Negro Pizzorno
PRODUCER: Fernando Costanza
ACCOUNT DIRECTOR: Eugenia Slosse,
Maria Laura de Rosa
CLIENT: Bayer
COUNTRY: Argentina

SMELL IS POWER
WIEDEN+KENNEDY
TV/Film | Television Commercial

EXECUTIVE CREATIVE DIRECTOR:
Susan Hoffman, Mark Fitzloff
CREATIVE DIRECTOR: Jason Bagley,
Craig Allen
ART DIRECTOR: Croix Gagnon
COPYWRITER: Nathaniel Lawlor,
Andy Laugenour
DIRECTOR OF PHOTOGRAPHY: Eli Born
DIRECTOR: Tim Heidecker, Eric Wareheim
EDITOR: Eric Notarnicola
EXECUTIVE PRODUCER: Dave Kneebone

PRODUCER: Lindsay Reed, Dale Nichols
LINE PRODUCER: Joshua Cohen
PRODUCTION COMPANY:
Absolutely Productions
VISUAL EFFECTS: The Mill
SOUND DESIGN: Eric Notarnicola,
Rohan Young
ACCOUNT DIRECTOR: Jessica Monsey
CLIENT: Old Spice
COUNTRY: United States

NOTHING BUT POTENTIAL
LEO BURNETT TORONTO
Broadcast Craft | Copywriting

CHIEF CREATIVE OFFICER: Judy John
CREATIVE DIRECTOR: Judy John,
Lisa Greenberg
ART DIRECTOR: Anthony Chelvanathan
COPYWRITER: Steve Persico
PHOTOGRAPHER: Frank Hoedl
DIRECTOR: Laurence Thrush
EDITOR: Mariam Fahmy (Panic&Bob)
HEAD OF PRODUCTION: Franca Piacente

PRODUCER: Franca Piacente,
Gladys Bachand, Kim Burchiel
PRODUCTION COMPANY: Suneeva
MUSIC/COMPOSER: Grayson Matthews
ACCOUNT DIRECTOR: Natasha Dagenais
ART BUYER: Leila Courey
CLIENT: Raising The Roof
COUNTRY: Canada

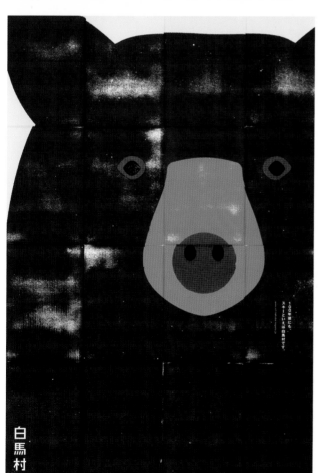

HAKUBA VILLAGE
SHINMURA DESIGN OFFICE
Poster or Billboard | Promotional

ART DIRECTOR: Norito Shinmura
COPYWRITER: Hiroyuki Nakazaki
DESIGNER: Kosuke Niwano
ILLUSTRATOR: Kosuke Niwano
CLIENT: Hakuba Village
COUNTRY: Japan

Advertising Merits

THE STORY YOU'RE IN TV CAMPAIGN
BBDO NEW YORK
TV/Film | Television Commercial

EXECUTIVE CREATIVE DIRECTOR: Greg Hahn,
Mike Smith
CHIEF CREATIVE OFFICER: David Lubars
ART DIRECTOR: Jaclyn Rink
COPYWRITER: Ashley Davis Marshall
DIRECTOR OF PHOTOGRAPHY: Jo Willems
DIRECTOR: Tom Kuntz
EDITOR: Steve Gandolfi, Joel Miller,
Isaac Chen, Georgia Dodson
EXECUTIVE PRODUCER: David Zander,
Jeff Scruton
LINE PRODUCER: Scott Kaplan
PRODUCTION COMPANY: MJZ
VISUAL EFFECTS: Framestore
SOUND DESIGN: Sound Lounge
ACCOUNT DIRECTOR: Tara Deveaux
CLIENT: HBO
COUNTRY: United States

HUSSARS
PUBLICIS CONSEIL
Broadcast Craft | Direction

CHAIRMAN: Arthur Sadoun
EXECUTIVE CREATIVE DIRECTOR:
Olivier Altmann
CHIEF CREATIVE OFFICER: Olivier Altmann
CREATIVE DIRECTOR: Olivier Desmettre,
Fabrice Delacourt
ART DIRECTOR: Philippe Boucheron
COPYWRITER: Patrice Lucet
DIRECTOR OF PHOTOGRAPHY:
Glynn Speeckaert
DIRECTOR: Antoine Bardou Jacquet
EDITOR: Bill Smedley
HEAD OF PRODUCTION: Muriel Allegrini (WAM)
EXECUTIVE PRODUCER:
Marc Fuentes (Partizan)
PRODUCER: Georges Bermann,
Frederic Genest
PRODUCTION COMPANY: Partizan
SOUND DESIGN: Laurent Favard,
Clemens Hourriere, sons in fx
PROJECT MANAGER: Jean-Patrick Chiquiar,
Valérie Henaff
ACCOUNT DIRECTOR: Marie Wallet
ART BUYER: Jean-Luc Chirio, Aurélie Lubot
CLIENT: ORANGE
COUNTRY: France

MADE OF MORE
ABBOTT MEAD VICKERS BBDO
Broadcast Craft | Cinematography

EXECUTIVE CREATIVE DIRECTOR:
Paul Brazier
CREATIVE DIRECTOR: Paul Brazier
ART DIRECTOR: Paul Brazier
COPYWRITER: Paul Brazier
DIRECTOR: Tom Hooper
EDITOR: Paul Watts, Bruce Townsend
EXECUTIVE PRODUCER: Yvonne Chalkley
PRODUCER: Molly Pope
PRODUCTION COMPANY: INFINITY
CLIENT: Guinness
COUNTRY: United Kingdom

SUMMER SALE
DDB LONDON
Press | Newspaper
Consumer Advertisement

EXECUTIVE CREATIVE DIRECTOR:
Grant Parker
ART DIRECTOR: Victor Monclus
COPYWRITER: Will Lowe
DESIGNER: Steve Sanderson, Greg Chapman
PHOTOGRAPHER: Frederike Helwig
ACCOUNT DIRECTOR: Paul Billingsley,
Charlotte Evans
ART BUYER: Sarah Thompson
CLIENT: Harvey Nichols
COUNTRY: United Kingdom

LOOK TWICE
JUNG VON MATT AG
Press | Magazine
Consumer Advertisement

VICE CHAIRMAN: Peter Figge
EXECUTIVE CREATIVE DIRECTOR:
Doerte Spengler-Ahrens, Jan Rexhausen
CREATIVE DIRECTOR: Felix Fenz
SENIOR ART DIRECTOR: Alexander Norvilas
ART DIRECTOR: Michael Hess
COPYWRITER: David Wegener
ILLUSTRATOR: Jesús González Rodríguez
PHOTOGRAPHER: Klaus Merz
EDITOR: Thomas Thiessen
PRODUCER: Philipp Wenhold
PHOTO EDITOR: Amina Warscheid,
Marius Schwiegk
PROJECT MANAGER: Julia Schreiber,
Ann-Kathrin Geertz
ACCOUNT DIRECTOR: Raphael Brinkert,
Sven Doerrenbaecher
ART BUYER: Madeleine von Hohenthal,
Bianca Winter
CLIENT: Daimler AG
COUNTRY: Germany

BALLOONS
LODUCCA
TV/Film | Television Commercial

CREATIVE DIRECTOR: Guga Ketzer,
Cassio Moron, Pedro Guerra, Marco Monteiro
ART DIRECTOR: Guga Ketzer, Andre Faria,
Dulcidio Caldeira
COPYWRITER: Guga Ketzer, Andre Faria,
Dulcidio Caldeira
ILLUSTRATOR: Daniel Semanas
DIRECTOR OF PHOTOGRAPHY:
Alexandre Ermel
ANIMATOR: Daniel Semanas
DIRECTOR: Dulcidio Caldeira
EXECUTIVE PRODUCER: Egisto Betti,
Ana Luisa Andre, Sid Fernandes
PRODUCER: Karina Vadasz
PRODUCTION COMPANY: Paranoid BR
SOUND DESIGN: Raw Produtora de Audio
MUSIC: William Tell Overture
COMPOSER: Gioachino Rossini
ACCOUNT DIRECTOR: Carmen Assumpção,
Sabrina Spinelli
CLIENT: MTV Brasil
COUNTRY: Brazil

GAME SIGNATURES
GPY&R MELBOURNE
Poster or Billboard | Promotional

EXECUTIVE CREATIVE DIRECTOR:
Ben Coulson
ART DIRECTOR: Chris Northam
COPYWRITER: Evan Roberts
PRODUCER: Gene Kingi
ACCOUNT DIRECTOR: Michael Napolitano
CLIENT: Australian Football League
COUNTRY: Australia

JAMESON LEGEND
TBWA\CHIAT\DAY, NEW YORK
Poster or Billboard | Transit

CHAIRMAN: Mark Figliulo
CHIEF CREATIVE OFFICER: Mark Figliulo
CREATIVE DIRECTOR: Jonathan Mackler,
Alisa Sengel Wixom, Kris Wixom
ART DIRECTOR: Anthony DeCarolis,
Kevin Kaminishi, John Clement
COPYWRITER: Alisa Sengel Wixom,
Erik Fahrenkopf, Dan Giachetti,
Kevin Kaminishi, Yusuke Toyoda, Aaron Stern
ILLUSTRATOR: Warren Change, Domenick
D'Andrea, Steven Levin
HEAD OF PRODUCTION: Robert Valdes
PRODUCER: Katherine D'Addario, John LaFaso
RETOUCHER: Erwin Brown, Daniel Finn,
Nancy Shaw, Randy Hiken
TYPOGRAPHER: I Love Dust
PROJECT MANAGER: Mimma Aliberti
ACCOUNT DIRECTOR: Lyndsey Corona
ART BUYER: Julia Menassa
CLIENT: Jameson
COUNTRY: United States

UNDERHEARD IN NEW YORK
BBH NEW YORK
Media Innovation |
Ambient/Environmental

CREATIVE DIRECTOR: Jessica Shriftman,
Zac Sax
ART DIRECTOR: Willy Wang
COPYWRITER: Rosemary Melchior
DESIGNER: Brian Moore
PROJECT MANAGER: Robert Weeks
ACCOUNT DIRECTOR: Dane Larsen
CLIENT: New York City Rescue Mission
COUNTRY: United States

UNICEF: GOOD SHIRTS
BBH NEW YORK
Media Innovation |
Ambient/Environmental

EXECUTIVE CREATIVE DIRECTOR: Ari Weiss
CHIEF CREATIVE OFFICER: John Patroulis
ART DIRECTOR: Dave Brown, Ian Hart
COPYWRITER: Dave Brown, Ian Hart
DESIGNER: Christine Gignac, Justin Gignac
ACCOUNT DIRECTOR: Kath Horton
CLIENT: UNICEF
COUNTRY: United States

INTERRUPTIONS
Y&R ARGENTINA
Press | Newspaper
Consumer Advertisement

EXECUTIVE CREATIVE DIRECTOR:
Martin Mercado
CREATIVE DIRECTOR: Diego Tuya, Dario Rial,
Martin Goldberg, Daniel Oliveira
ART DIRECTOR: Gonzalo Fernandez
COPYWRITER: Juan Ignacio Galardi
PHOTOGRAPHER: El Negro Pizzorno
PRODUCER: Fernando Costanza
ACCOUNT DIRECTOR: Eugenia Slosse,
Maria Laura de Rosa
CLIENT: Bayer
COUNTRY: Argentina

NIGHT VIEW ASSIST
BBDO PROXIMITY BERLIN GMBH
Press | Magazine
Consumer Advertisement

CHIEF CREATIVE OFFICER: Jan Harbeck,
David Mously, Wolfgang Schneider
ART DIRECTOR: Daniel Haschtmann
COPYWRITER: David Missing
PHOTOGRAPHER: Jan van Endert
PRODUCER: Philipp Wenhold
POST-PRODUCTION:
Sevengreen Picture Works GmbH, Hamburg
TYPOGRAPHER: Daniel Haschtmann
MANAGING DIRECTOR:
Dirk Spakowski (MARK BBDO Praha)
ACCOUNT DIRECTOR: Sebastian Schlosser,
Jan Hendrick Oelckers, Martin Vejdovsky,
Jana Valencikova (MARK BBDO Praha)
ACCOUNT MANAGER: Joris Jonker,
Ann-Cathrin von Rechenberg
ART BUYER: Lynn Sutliff
AGENCY: BBDO Germany GmbH
CLIENT: Mercedes-Benz Ceská republika s.r.o.
COUNTRY: Germany

TRANSFERTYPE
ALMAPBBDO
Press | Magazine Insert

EXECUTIVE CREATIVE DIRECTOR:
Marcello Serpa
CHIEF CREATIVE OFFICER: Luiz Sanches
CREATIVE DIRECTOR: Luiz Sanches
ART DIRECTOR: Marcos Medeiros
COPYWRITER: Andre Kassu
ILLUSTRATOR: Marcos Medeiros
CLIENT: Billboard Brasil
COUNTRY: Brazil

LITTLE MARINA
MOTHER NEW YORK
Ambient/Environmental | Large Scale

CLIENT: Target
COUNTRY: United States

Integrated is tougher than ever.

Keep fighting the good fight.

This was a bad idea.

As a new category for the ADC Awards, our Jury felt the challenge two-fold. Each notable entry discussion became part of a larger dialogue on the merits of the category itself. Should this be a category? And how does it work?

We found the merit there. Putting a lens to the 30,000-foot view is more important than ever in this era of seemingly infinite creative opportunity and large-scale and diverse collaborations.

And frankly, a lot of work with beautiful pieces looked incomplete or uneven from that perspective. It was our intent to recognize campaigns that not only had a strong idea and narrative, but ones that treated each touch point uniquely within a comprehensive structure. The design of each individual execution in the campaigns selected has a life of its own. And as a group, we think they work in wildly different ways.

Our intent was to showcase collective quality over quantity, and orchestration over aggregation. We hope these pieces set a proper course and are excited to see the space continue to develop and mature.

Brian Dilorenzo
Integrated Jury Chair

Integrated

Integrated Jury

Brian Dilorenzo
McCann Erickson New York
United States

Aaron Padin
JWT New York
United States

Kristen Cahill
@radical.media
United States

Scott Vitrone
Wieden+Kennedy New York
United States

John Cornette
Saatchi & Saatchi New York
United States

Steve Wax
Ladies & Gentlemen
United States

Bobby Hershfield
Mother New York
United States

Faris Yakob
MDC Partners, kbs+,
Spies&Assassins
United States

ACTIVATE
THE FUTURE

HOME   EVALUATION   DOCUMENTARY   ABOUT   FORUM   **ELECTRONAUT**

WELCOME **ANDREAS BAUMERT**   Help shape the future of mobility   SIGN OU

ANDREAS BAUMERT

I DRIVE A **GAS VEHICLE**   ▾

10,000

YOUR SOCIAL IMPACT SCORE

32

SPREAD THE NUMBERS f t

MY SOCIAL IMPACT   **MY PERSONAL IMPACT**   MY EV RANGE

ANNUAL CO2 EMISSIONS

2,427 lbs

The BMW ActiveE offers emission-free exhilaration.

ANNUAL SAVINGS

$1,297

Not only does switching to a BMW EV help preserve our wonderful planet, it also puts some extra cash back in your wallet.

CARBON FOOTPRINT SAVED

21% FOOTPRINT SAVINGS

79% REMAINING FOOTPRINT

AVERAGE FUEL PRICES

GAS $3.57

DIESEL $3.79

BARRELS OF FUEL NOT USED

13

That's enough to fill 11 bathtubs.

THINK OF YOUR CO2 EMISSIONS THIS WAY:

9,574 HOURS

of running your lawnmower. Your neighbors might get annoyed.

WHAT CAN YOU BUY WITH YOUR SAVINGS

649

cups of your morning java. That'll put some goose bumps in your drive.

A FULL TANK OF GAS VS EV

$64.22 $11.89

GAS   EV

See how much it costs to drive an EV the same distance as one full tank of fuel.

TRIPS TO THE GAS PUMP SAVED

29

That's 4.8 hours that can be spent anywhere but the gas station.

AVERAGE % OF BATTERY USED EACH DAY

14% COMMUTE

86% REMAINING

14% of a BMW ActiveE battery only takes 1 hour(s) to charge. Plug it in overnight and start each day with a "full tank"

 SIGN UP FOR UPDATES

 GET THE BMW EVolve MOBILE APP

 EXPERIENCE THE BMW ActiveE

› BATTERIES

100% ELEC

› RANGE

European model sh

ONE CAR. TWO SOULS.

The next step in the future of mobility is anything but just another electric car.

The high-performance thrills and unrivaled efficiency you've come to expect from The Ultimate Driving Machine®.

WE'RE GOING TO NEED

Electronauts

ACTIVATE THE FUTURE

HOME   EVALUATION   DOCUMENTARY   ABOUT   FORUM

WELCOME TO **ACTIVATE THE FUTURE**   Get a BMW EValuation to see how an EV could impact your life

THE TRUE POWER OF AN ELECTRIC VEHICLE

EXPLORE THE IMPACT IN YOUR BMW EValuation

BMW EVs offer the power and performance expected of an Ultimate Driving Machine®. But their true power will be measured in the way they change lives. Welcome to BMW's EValuation, where we analyze how you, your facebook friends, and the world around you all benefit from driving EVs.

▸ START YOUR EVALUATION

WANT TO BE A BMW ELECTRONAUT?
▸ WATCH VIDEO

 SIGN UP FOR UPDATES   GET THE BMW EVolve MOBILE APP   EXPER

Share on: +1 59   👍 Like   f 4,127 people like this.

▸ Disclaimer   ▸ Support   ▸ Privacy Policy & Legal

WHEREVER YOU WANT TO GO

FOUR FILMS ABOUT THE FUTURE OF MOBILITY.

▸ WATCH THE TRAILER   ▸ CAST BIOS

BUZZ ALDRIN - ASTRONAUT
CHRIS ANDERSON - EDITOR-IN-CHIEF, WIRED MAGAZINE
CHRIS BROGAN - PRESIDENT AND CEO, HUMAN BUSINESS WORKS
LAWRENCE BURNS - CO-AUTHOR, "REINVENTING THE AUTOMOBILE"
ROBIN CHASE - CO-FOUNDER AND FORMER CEO, ZIPCAR & GOLOCO
PROF. WAI CHENG - DIRECTOR MIT SLOAN AUTOMOTIVE LAB
GRAHAM HILL - FOUNDER, TREEHUGGER.COM
RICHARD MATTILA - GENZYME CORPORATION
MARISSA MAYER - VP OF CONSUMER PRODUCTS, GOOGLE
SYD MEAD - VISUAL FUTURIST
MIKE MUSTO - EDITOR-IN-CHIEF, RIDELUST.COM
LAURENZ SCHAFFER - PRESIDENT BMW GROUP DESIGNWORKSUSA
NAVEEN SELVADURAI - CO-FOUNDER, FOURSQUARE
GEORGE WHITESIDES - CEO, VIRGIN GALACTIC

YOUR ENVIRONMENTAL IMPACT
Think of your vehicle's annual emissions this way:
To offset the damage of 9,360 lbs. of CO_2, you'd have to plant 21 trees annually.

BASED ON 12K MILES ANNUALLY

BMW ACTIVEE - A SOCIAL EXPERIMENT SHAPING THE FUTURE OF MOBILITY
KIRSHENBAUM BOND SENECAL + PARTNERS

CHAIRMAN & CEO: Lori Senecal (kbs+)
PRESIDENT: Ed Brojerdi (kbs+)
CHIEF CREATIVE OFFICER: Ed Brojerdi, Izzy DeBellis (kbs+)
CREATIVE DIRECTOR: Marc Hartzman, Will Bright, Faris Yakob, Anthony Monahan (kbs+)
SENIOR ART DIRECTOR: Peter Mendez (kbs+)
ART DIRECTOR: Andreas Baumert, Jon Cochran, Lance Parrish (kbs+)
COPYWRITER: Ash Tavassoli, Leah Alfonso (kbs+)
ANIMATOR: Prologue Pictures, Valins & Co.
DIRECTOR: Kurt Mattila (Prologue Pictures)
EDITOR: Jason Webb, Rob Auten, Kurt Mattila, Oliver Hecks, Ly Chung (kbs+)
CHIEF INFORMATION OFFICER: Matt Powell (kbs+)
DIRECTOR, CONTENT PRODUCTION: Dominic Ferro (kbs+)
EXECUTIVE PRODUCER: Alexander Dervin (Prologue Pictures)
SENIOR PRODUCER: Brooke Kaylor (kbs+)
CONTENT PRODUCER: Craig Shuster (kbs+)
PRODUCER: Brian Hall, Christina Hwang (Prologue Pictures)
PRODUCTION COMPANY: Prologue Pictures
SOUND MIXER: Gabriel Moffat (Prologue Pictures)
DIRECTOR OF WEB TECHNOLOGY: Rana Dutt (kbs+)
DIRECTOR OF INTERACTION DESIGN: Jed McClure (kbs+)
INTERACTION DESIGNERS: Mustafa Bagdatli, Victor Zambrano (kbs+)
MOBILE DEVELOPERS: Doug Strittmatter, Marc Brown, Jason McKim, Mike Reed, Alan Garcia, Michael Nieves, Jay Leonov, Rajeev Gupta (kbs+)
EXECUTIVE TECHNICAL PRODUCER: Nick Meyer (kbs+)
SENIOR TECHNICAL PRODUCER: Dennis Hanley (kbs+)
TECHNICAL PRODUCERS: Ken Kobel, Peter Tierney (kbs+)
DIRECTOR OF DIGITAL ENGAGEMENT: Tom Buontempo (kbs+)
GROUP ACCOUNT DIRECTOR: Katie Klumper (kbs+)
ACCOUNT DIRECTOR: David Solomito (kbs+)
ACCOUNT EXECUTIVE: Jason Flynn (kbs+)
SOCIAL MARKETING & COMMUNITY MANAGER: Matt Musick (kbs+)
SENIOR BRAND STRATEGIST: James Thorpe (kbs+)
CLIENT: BMW North America
COUNTRY: United States

Sprint *All. Together. Now.*

4,236 forwards

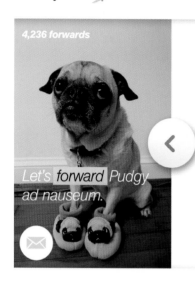

Let's *forward* Pudgy
ad nauseum.

Welcome to
Random acts
of togetherness.

When you're truly Unlimited, you can text, web
and call to your heart's content without worries.
Let's see what we can all do together.

Let's *wish* Veatrice
happy birthday

America's favorite 4G Network.

True Unlimited *text, Web and calling.*

Show me the plan   Show me the devices

0:06 / 0:10

(816) 892-5407
VeatriceH@gmail.com

You **Tube** | Search | Browse   Upload   Create Account   Si

SPRINT ALL TOGETHER NOW
GOODBY, SILVERSTEIN & PARTNERS

CHAIRMAN: Rich Silverstein, Jeff Goodby
EXECUTIVE CREATIVE DIRECTOR:
Christian Haas, Jamie Barrett
ART DIRECTOR: Aaron Dietz, Kevin Koller,
Felipe Lima, Maggie Bradshaw, Juan Saucedo
COPYWRITER: Mandy Dietz, Rus Chao,
Toria Emery, Carter Debski, Lesly Waggoner
DIRECTOR OF PHOTOGRAPHY: Scott Buttfield
EDITOR: Mahoko Kuramasu
HEAD OF PRODUCTION: Cindy Fluitt,
Carey Head
EXECUTIVE PRODUCER: Carey Crosby,
Jeremy Adirim, TJ Kearney, Tom Ruge
PRODUCER: Kat Friis, Rob Sondik,
Taryn Waggoner, Gianni Argiris,
Mia Ruiz-Escoto, Cheryl Rosenthal
PRODUCTION COMPANY: Grow Interactive,
E Films
VISUAL EFFECTS: Mike Landry e-films, E Level
SOUND DESIGN: Human, Barking Owl
PROJECT MANAGER: Jennifer Pao,
Frannie Rhodes, Britney Weaver,
Jason Cappiello
ACCOUNT DIRECTOR: Rob Smith,
Michael Chase, Amanda Andriesz
CLIENT: Sprint
COUNTRY: United States

ICE CUBE CELEBRATES THE EAMES

CELEBRATE THE ERA THAT CONTINUES TO INSPIRE THE WORLD: ART IN L.A. 1945–1980

OCT 2011 TO APR 2012
pacificstandardtime.org

PACIFIC
STANDARD
TIME

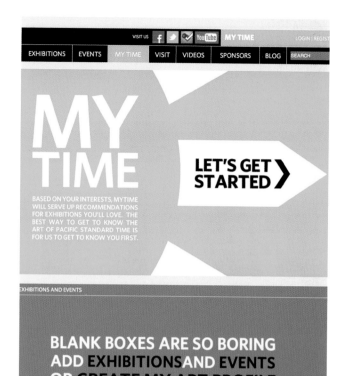

CELEBRATE THE ERA
TBWA\CHIAT\DAY, LOS ANGELES

EXECUTIVE CREATIVE DIRECTOR:
Patrick O'Neill
CREATIVE DIRECTOR: Jayanta Jenkins
ART DIRECTOR: Stephen Lum,
Jeremiah Wassom
COPYWRITER: Evan Brown, Liz Cartwright
DESIGNER: Lori McMichael,
Jason Fryer, Bory Chung
DIRECTOR OF PHOTOGRAPHY: Paul Ryan
DIRECTOR: Dave Meyers, Jesse Dylan
EDITOR: Chris Davis, Al Kamalizad
HEAD OF PRODUCTION: Richard O'Neill,
Chincha Evans
EXECUTIVE PRODUCER: Guia Iacomin,
Frank Scherma, Jim Bouvet, Priscilla Cohen
PRODUCER: Christopher Spencer,
Micah Kawaguchi-Ailetcher, Lacy Plunk,
Hillary Rogers, Kacey Harahan, Matt Benson
PRODUCTION COMPANY:
@radical.media, Wondros
VISUAL EFFECTS: Kim Stevenson,
Julie Lenoble
SOUND DESIGN: Dean Hovey, Brian Angely
MUSIC/COMPOSER: Paul Bessenbacher
PROJECT MANAGER: Heather Kuhn
ACCOUNT DIRECTOR: Mike Litwin
ART BUYER: Karen Youngs
DESIGN INTERN: Donny Smith
CLIENT: Pacific Standard Time
COUNTRY: United States

THE FACE OF THE MARATHON
HEIMAT

EXECUTIVE CREATIVE DIRECTOR:
Guido Heffels
CREATIVE DIRECTOR: Ove Gley, Ole Vinck,
Guido Heffels
DESIGN DIRECTOR: Ove Gley
ART DIRECTOR: Patrick Düver, Timm Holm
COPYWRITER: Dominik Maas, David Kauder,
Ole Vinck
DESIGNER: Franziska Kriehn, Lucas Schneider
DIRECTOR OF PHOTOGRAPHY:
ACNE Production (Berlin/Stockholm)
EDITOR: Niels Münter
EXECUTIVE PRODUCER: Jessica Valin
PRODUCER: Niels Münter
PRODUCTION COMPANY:
ACNE Production (Berlin/Stockholm)
VISUAL EFFECTS:
Swedish Chameleon (Stockholm)
SOUND DESIGN: Dinahmoe (Stockholm)
PROJECT MANAGER: Julia Bubenik,
Florian Hoffmann, Nico Buchholz
ACCOUNT DIRECTOR:
Matthias von Bechtolsheim
CLIENT: adidas AG
COUNTRY: Germany

INTERACTIVE
Website | Campaign Site

THE BEST EXCUSE EVER
Norte

INSIGHT
Usually, when a man wants to go to the bar to have a beer with his friends, a girlfriend pops up with a different plan, like tickets for the theatre or dinner with her parents.

STRATEGY
Since a good deed is the only excuse that's impossible to refuse, we used it as a tool to help boyfriends go to the bar without having to hear a single complaint from their girlfriends.

SOLUTION
For each Norte beer boyfriends had at the bar, the brand allotted 1 minute of good deeds. And a group of Norte workers carried out the tasks.

1 FOR EACH NORTE BEER BOYFRIENDS HAD AT THE BAR

1 BOTTLE TOP = 1 MINUTE OF GOOD DEEDS

005048 MINUTOS

2 NORTE ALLOTTED 1 MINUTE OF GOOD DEEDS.

3 A TEAM OF WORKERS WERE IN CHARGE OF REFURBISHING SCHOOLS, PLANTING TREES, RESTORING MONUMENTS, IMPROVING PARKS AND CLEANING UP LAKES.

4 THIS IS HOW GIRLFRIENDS WERE UNABLE TO GET MAD WHEN THEIR BOYFRIENDS WENT TO THE BAR.

RESULTS
50,043 minutes accrued for the making of good deeds. The minutes were used to:

Repair schools

Plant trees

Restore monuments

Improve parks

And clean up lakes.

AND THE MOST IMPORTANT PART:

WE MADE IT POSSIBLE FOR BOYFRIENDS TO GO TO THE BAR TROUBLE FREE.

THE BEST EXCUSE EVER
DEL CAMPO NAZCA SAATCHI & SAATCHI

EXECUTIVE CREATIVE DIRCTOR: Maxi Itzkoff,
Mariano Serkin
CREATIVE DIRECTOR: Fernando Militerno
ART DIRECTOR: Maxi Borrego
COPYWRITER: Diego Gueler
DIRECTOR OF PHOTOGRAPHY: Leandro Filloy
DIRECTOR: Felipe&Pancho
EDITOR: Mauro Carpinacci
HEAD OF PRODUCTION: Adrian Aspani
AGENCY PRODUCER: Camilo Rojas,
Lucas Delenikas
PRODUCTION COMPANY: Primo Buenos Aires
MUSIC/COMPOSER: Supercharango
ACCOUNT DIRECTOR: Jaime Vidal,
Patricia Abelenda
CLIENT: AbInBev/ Norte Beer
COUNTRY: Argentina

MINI BEST TEST DRIVE. EVER. PERIOD
BUTLER, SHINE, STERN & PARTNERS

CREATIVE DIRECTOR: Steve Mapp, Lyle Yetman
ART DIRECTOR: Christian Laniosz
COPYWRITER: Erik Enberg
DIRECTOR OF PHOTOGRAPHY: Mark Plummer
DIRECTOR: Erich Joiner
EDITOR: Peter Koob
HEAD OF PRODUCTION: Brian Latt
PRODUCER: Joby Ochsner (Tool),
Stacy McClain (BSSP)
PRODUCTION COMPANY: Tool of North America
VISUAL EFFECTS: The Mission
SOUND DESIGN: Squekeclean
CLIENT: MINI USA
COUNTRY: United States

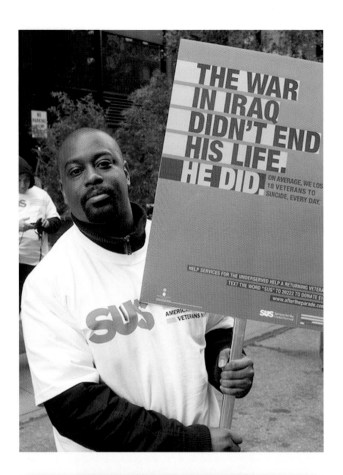

AFTER THE PARADE
JWT NEW YORK

EXECUTIVE CREATIVE DIRECTOR:
Aaron Padin
CHIEF CREATIVE OFFICER: Peter Nicholson
CREATIVE DIRECTOR: Dave Wasserman
ART DIRECTOR: Jay Wee, Ben Morejon
COPYWRITER: Vahbiz Engineer,
Rachel Birnbaum, Alexis Read, Alex Schaeffer
DESIGNER: Akira Nakamura, TJ Zafarana
PLANNER: Anna Bradfield
PHOTOGRAPHER: Joey L., Hugo Fitzgerald
DIRECTOR: Brams Coppens (Welcome Home)
EDITING PRODUCER: Meagan Carroll
EDITOR: Tony Change, Ian Mackenzie,
Nick Divers
EDITING HOUSE: JWTwo, Mackenzie Cutler
EXECUTIVE PRODUCER: Angela Buck
POST PRODUCTION EXECUTIVE PRODUCER:
Sarah Hesterman
PRINT PRODUCER: Melanie Magatelli
FLAME: Marcus Wood
COLORIST: Ricky Gausis
PRODUCTION COMPANY: Caviar Content,
Fixer Films (Welcome Home)

POST PRODUCTION (VISUAL EFFECTS): MPC NY
POST PRODUCTION PRODUCER (VISUAL EFFECTS):
Derek Macleod
SOUND DESIGN: Alan Friedman, Andy Green,
Eugene Cho
MIXER: Mike Jansson
MUSIC PRODUCER: Michelle Curran, Jennie Armon
MUSIC SUPERVISOR: Michael Perri
MUSIC: Amber
COMPOSER: Dennis Mccarthy, Jerome Rossi
SOUND: Sam Shaffer
STUDIO: JWT S05
RADIO PRODUCER: Craig Canigilia, Paul Greco
PROJECT MANAGER: Lindsey Allen
MANAGER: Greg Tiefenbrun
ACCOUNT DIRECTOR: Drew Train, Beth Miller,
Ryan Gardiner
ART BUYER: Sara Clark
CLIENT: Services for the Underserved
COUNTRY: United States

THE VOICELESS CAMPAIGN
TBWA\HUNT\LASCARIS,
JOHANNESBURG

EXECUTIVE CREATIVE DIRECTOR:
Damon Stapleton
CHIEF CREATIVE OFFICER: John Hunt
SENIOR ART DIRECTOR: Shelley Smoler
ART DIRECTOR: Shelley Smoler
COPYWRITER: Raphael Basckin
COPY EDITOR: Raphael Basckin
PHOTOGRAPHER: James Oatway,
Robin Hammond, Dirk-Jan Visser
PRODUCER: Craig Walker
RETOUCHER: Rob Frew
PROJECT MANAGER: Kershnee Pillay
ACCOUNT DIRECTOR: Bridget Langley
ART BUYER: Simone Allem
CLIENT: The Zimbabwean Newspaper
COUNTRY: South Africa

28 DAY PERSECUTION OF
ROMMY GULLA
THE CAMPAIGN PALACE

CHIEF CREATIVE OFFICER: Reed Collins
CREATIVE DIRECTOR: Gerhard Myburgh
SENIOR ART DIRECTOR: Gerhard Myburgh
COPYWRITER: Hywel James
DESIGNER: Samantha Hornitsky
PRODUCER: Stefan Puskar, Warwick Boulter
PRODUCTION COMPANY: Film Construction
DIGITAL AGENCY: Suede
ACCOUNT DIRECTOR: Toby McKinnon
CLIENT: Panasonic Australia Pty Ltd
COUNTRY: Australia

SCREW*D
Y&R CHICAGO

CHIEF CREATIVE OFFICER: Bob Winter
CREATIVE DIRECTOR: Jon Eckman
ASSOCIATE CREATIVE DIRECTOR:
Richard Fischer, Evan Thompson
ART DIRECTOR: Richard Fischer
COPYWRITER: Evan Thompson
DESIGNER: Thomas Nicholas, Optimus
INTERACTIVE DIRECTOR: Grant Skinner,
Matt Ogers
EDITOR: Mark Panik (Don't Panik!)
HEAD OF PRODUCTION: Brian Smego
HEAD OF DIGITAL: Matt Witt
PRODUCER: Kara Pierce
PRODUCTION COMPANY: Tool
MUSIC/COMPOSER: Beta Patrol
ACCOUNT DIRECTOR: Kevin Babcock
ACCOUNT SUPERVISOR: Priya Bordia
CLIENT: Craftsman
COUNTRY: United States

Integrated Merits

A WORLD-CLASS LOCAL
FORSMAN & BODENFORS

ART DIRECTOR: Staffan Forsman,
Lars Johansson, Ferhat Deniz Fors
COPYWRITER: Anders Hegerfors,
Elisabeth Christensson
DESIGNER: Staffan Håkanson
PRODUCTION COMPANY:
Thomson Interactive Media
ACCOUNT DIRECTOR:
Ann Spennare Bengtsson
ADVERTISER'S SUPERVISOR: Åse Henell,
Nicola Magnusson
CLIENT: Göteborgs-Posten Newspaper
COUNTRY: Sweden

EVERYDAY RIDER SPONSORSHIPS
LEO BURNETT MELBOURNE

EXECUTIVE CREATIVE DIRECTOR:
Jason Williams
ART DIRECTOR: Justin Nagorcka
COPYWRITER: Sarah McGregor
ACCOUNT DIRECTOR: Patrick Rowe
CLIENT: Giant Bikes
COUNTRY: Australia

MEAN STINKS
LEO BURNETT CHICAGO

GLOBAL CHIEF CREATIVE OFFICER:
Mark Tutssel
EXECUTIVE CREATIVE DIRECTOR:
Becky Swanson
CHIEF CREATIVE OFFICER: Susan Credle
CREATIVE DIRECTOR: Clay Black
ART DIRECTOR: Sarah Block, Hmi Hmi Gibbs,
Yumi Minamikurosawa, Chris Rodriguez
COPYWRITER: AJ Hassan, Matt Miller,
Eric Routenberg, David Schermer,
Craig Shparago
DESIGNER: Eing Omathikul, Alisa Wolfson,
Andrea Lyons
PHOTOGRAPHER: Brian Sorg
EXECUTIVE PRODUCER: David L. Moore
PRODUCER: Laurie Gustafson,
Bonnie Van Steen
DIGITAL PARTNER: IMC2
ACCOUNT DIRECTOR: Anne Rockey,
Sarah Bogaczyk
CLIENT: P&G Secret
COUNTRY: United States

Being a student is tougher than ever.

Keep fighting the good fight.

ArtDirectorsClub

---

zufällig in Posen, rauchend und sinnierend, die denen der Künstler sehr ähneln – wobei wohl offenbleiben muss, wer hier wen beeinflusste. Dass der Künstler schon in den Goldenen Zwanzigern als Stilikone gefeiert wurde, lässt sich auch an den Themen der damaligen Kinofilme ablesen: Der Regisseur King Vidor verfilmte 1926 z.B. die Pariser Quartier-Latin-Romanze „La Bohème" mit den Stummfilmstars John Gilbert und Lilian Gish. Das beliebte Genre der Maler-und-Modell-Story wurde gleich mehrfach bearbeitet und nicht zufällig auch das Leben des Beau Brummell 1924 mit dem schönen John Barrymore auf der Leinwand verewigt.[10]

Dass die Künstler der Avantgarden mit den Modedesignern ihrer Zeit Kontakt pflegten oder gar an gemeinsamen Entwürfen arbeiteten, muss vor diesem Hintergrund nicht mehr verwundern. Coco Chanel war mit Pablo Picasso, Jean Cocteau, Max Jacob, Sergei Djagilew und vielen anderen

unmittelbar befreundet und soll mit dem ausgesprochen eleganten Igor Strawinski (12) gar eine Affäre gehabt haben. Das einfache weiße Fischerhemd mit blauen Querstreifen, das seit dem berühmten Porträt von Robert Doisneau (13) gewissermaßen zu Picassos Markenzeichen wurde, hatte auch Coco Chanel in ihrer Mode bearbeitet. Sie trug es bereits 1930 auf dem für eine

Frau damals spektakulären Privatfoto, das sie in männlichem Habit zeigte (14). Andere Künstler wiederum zog es mehr zu Elsa Schiaparelli, jener anderen Grande Dame der Pariser Mode. Ihre Entwürfe sind von der Kunst der Surrealisten deutlich geprägt, sie entwarf 1938 zusammen mit Salvador Dalí das „Hummer-Kleid" und andere Kreationen, die seine Kunst zitierten, wie z.B. das „Schubladen-Kleid für die moderne Sekretärin", den „Schuh-Hut", das „Lippenkleid" oder den Parfumflakon in Form einer weiblichen Büste. Dass Dalí (15) selbst gerne mit seinem Äußeren spielte und es in Szene setzte, braucht wohl nicht eigens betont zu werden. Die Kooperationen der Künstler mit den Modehäusern und Modezeitschriften kamen letztlich beiden Parteien zugute: Wenn z.B. Giorgio de Chirico, der Apollinaire 1914 als antikisierende Büste mit modernem Sonnenbrillenaufsatz porträtierte (16),[11] auch Modezeichnungen für die Vogue anfertigte, wertete dies die Zeitschrift ebenso auf, wie es dem Bekanntheitsgrad des Künstlers half. Die neuartigen Selbstinszenierungen der Künstler vor der Kamera richteten sich jedenfalls immer gezielt an die Öffentlichkeit. Der Brauch, ein Porträtfoto von sich als repräsentative Visitenkarte zu verwenden, war bereits vor 1900 beliebt, so wie auch der Bildtyp des Atelierfotos bzw. des Künstlers bei der Arbeit schon seit der Romantik sehr verbreitet war. Bei den besprochenen Fotografien drängt sich zudem der Verdacht auf, dass die Künstler damit das Starfoto nachahmten, das die Berühmtheiten der Bühne und des Films signierten und an ihre Fangemeinden ver-

teilten. Denn mit Widmungen unterschriebene Künstlerfotografien finden sich in dieser Zeit häufig (11, 12).

Richten wir das Augenmerk eingehender auf die Gesten und Attitüden, Kleider und Accessoires: Mir scheint, die modische Pathosformel des modernen Künstlers lässt sich besser beschreiben als man angesichts der Heterogenität der Erscheinungen annehmen mag. Man könnte z.B. nach Künstlergruppen und Perioden vorgehen und feststellen, dass die frühen Surrealisten oft im eleganten Anzug auftraten, so dass sie ihre Körperlichkeit eher zurücknahmen – ganz im Gegensatz zum späteren Pablo Picasso oder Max Ernst (17), die sich auch gerne mit freiem Oberkörper zeigten, in freier Natur oder beim Malen im Atelier. Andere, wie z.B. Bertolt Brecht (18) oder Jean Genet (19), demonstrierten plakativ die Nähe zum Proletariat, mit dem sie sich auch in ihrer Literatur solidarisierten. Genets hochgekrempelte Ärmel zum offenen Hemd erinnern unmittelbar an das von ihm so häufig beschriebene Matrosen-Motiv. Die Expressionisten hingegen inszenierten sich

eher bescheiden, sie blieben, wie z.B. die Atelierbilder von Ernst Ludwig Kirchner zeigen, der älteren Tradition der Boheme verpflichtet.[12] Die Prägung durch den jeweiligen Künstlerkreis wird also stets sichtbar. Aber es lassen sich auch übergreifende Merkmale für den schönen Künstler der Moderne ausmachen, die erstaunlich beständig sind in ihrer Wiederkehr.

So könnte man z.B. von einer regelrechten Künstlerfrisur sprechen. Von Goethe und Schiller an zeigten sich die Intellektuellen gerne im Halbprofil und signalisierten durch das locker nach hinten gekämmte Haar eine hohe Stirn, die Grundvoraussetzung jeder Denkpose. Jene sich geschmeidig aufrichtende Stirnlocke zierte Stefan George (20), André Breton (21) und Jean Cocteau (22), sie war aber auch im Komponistenporträt beliebt – und kehrt in den Darstellungen eines Franz Schubert, Felix Mendelssohn Bartholdy, Gustav Mahler, Richard Wagner u.a. beständig wieder. Das aufwallende Haar zeugt von wahrem Genie und kraftvoller Virilität. Wer über die entsprechende Haarpracht nicht verfügt, kann seiner geistigen Radikalität aber auch durch eine absichtliche Glatze Ausdruck verleihen.

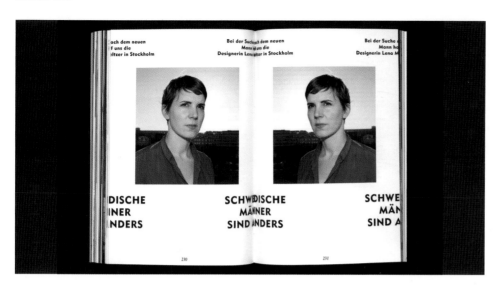

DER SCHÖNE MANN – DAS MAGAZIN
UNIVERSITY OF THE ARTS, BREMEN
DESIGN | Magazine Editorial | Full Issue

ART DIRECTOR: Professor Tania Prill
DESIGNER: Jeferson Brito Andrade,
Yamuna Peters, Josepha Brun,
Bianca Holtschke, Matthias Keller
DIRECTOR OF PHOTOGRAPHY:
Joachim Baldauf
EDITOR: Annette Geiger, Kai Lehmann,
Ursula Zillig
PUBLISHER: Textem Verlag, Hamburg
CLIENT: Annette Geiger, Kai Lehmann,
Ursula Zillig
COUNTRY: Germany

GET THE MESSAGE

HELPGUIDE.ORG

DRUG ABUSE PSA
"GET THE MESSAGE"
ART CENTER COLLEGE OF DESIGN
MOTION | Motion Graphics

ART DIRECTOR: Kevin Shin
COPYWRITER: Teodros Hailye, Lamson To,
Kevin Shin, Esther Park
DESIGNER: Teodros Hailye, Kevin Shin,
Esther Park, Lamson To
ILLUSTRATOR: Kevin Shin
ANIMATOR: Teodros Hailye, Kevin Shin,
Esther Park, Lamson To
SOUND DESIGN: Charles Gartner, Lamson To
VISUAL EFFECTS: Teodros Hailye
TYPOGRAPHER: Esther Park
COUNTRY: United States

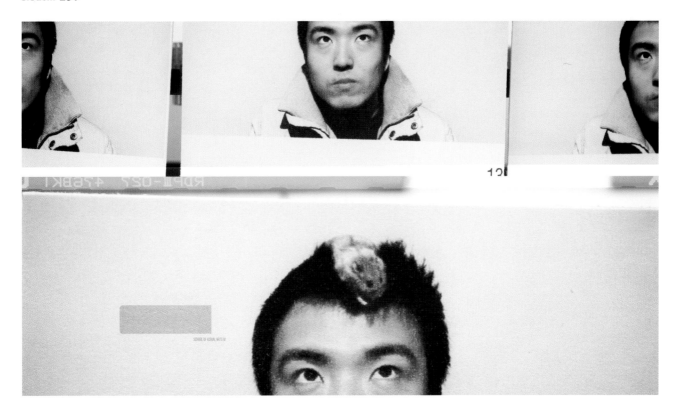

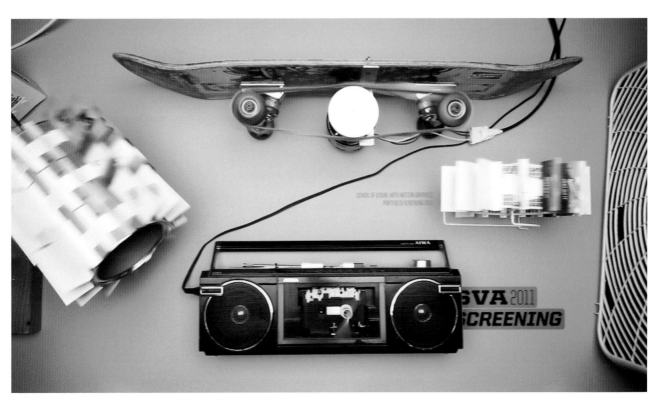

SVA PORTFOLIO SCREENING 2011
SCHOOL OF VISUAL ARTS
MOTION | TV Identities/Openings/Teasers

SENIOR ART DIRECTOR: Adam Grabowski
ANIMATOR: Adam Grabowski
HEAD OF PRODUCTION: Peter Grabowski
CLIENT: School of Visual Arts
COUNTRY: United States

EXORCIST
FILMACADEMY BADEN-WÜRTTEMBERG
ADVERTISING | Broadcast Craft | Art Direction

CREATIVE DIRECTOR: Andre Price
ART DIRECTOR: Andre Price
COPYWRITER: Andre Price
DIRECTOR OF PHOTOGRAPHY: Roland Stuprich
DIRECTOR: Andreas Roth
EDITOR: Alexander Menkö
EXECUTIVE PRODUCER:
Christian Hergenröther, Andreas Roth
PRODUCER: Christian Hergenröther
PRODUCTION COMPANY:
Filmakademie Baden-Württemberg
VISUAL EFFECTS: lafourmi postproduction
SOUND DESIGN: The German Wahnsinn Team
MUSIC/COMPOSER:
The German Wahnsinn Team
PUBLISHER: Rebecca Noeh
CLIENT: Dirt Devil
COUNTRY: Germany

SPREAD THE LOVE.

You know what you like. We know what you'll love. Just type in the name of your favorite song or artist
and we'll sort through our library of over 800,000 songs to create a station as unique as you are.

PANDORA®
internet radio

DON'T STOP 'TILL YOU GET ENOUGH

IMAGINE.

You know what you like. We know what you'll love. Just type in the name of your favorite song or artist
and we'll sort through our library of over 800,000 songs to create a station as unique as you are.

PANDORA
internet radio

You know what you like. We know what you'll love. Just type in the name of your favorite song or artist
and we'll sort through our library of over 800,000 songs to create a station as unique as you are.

PANDORA
internet radio

PANDORA POSTER SERIES
UNIVERSITY OF NORTH TEXAS
ADVERTISING | Poster or Billboard
Promotional

CREATIVE DIRECTOR: Bill Ford
ART DIRECTOR: Katie Johnson,
Antonio Mondragon
COPYWRITER: Katie Johnson,
Antonio Mondragon
CLIENT: Pandora Radio
COUNTRY: United States

Keep the Meter Running

a campaign
for the

HOMELESS YOUTH ALLIANCE
S.F. CA.

Art Director - Bennett Austin

Keep the Meter Running

HOMELESS YOUTH ALLIANCE
S.F. CA.

KEEP THE METER RUNNING
MIAMI AD SCHOOL (SAN FRANCISCO)
ADVERTISING | Ambient/Environmental
Stunts/Guerrilla

CREATIVE DIRECTOR: Steve Nathans
ART DIRECTOR: Bennett Austin
COPYWRITER: Bennett Austin
VISUAL EFFECTS: Tufan Guzeloglu
CLIENT: Homeless Youth Alliance
COUNTRY: United States

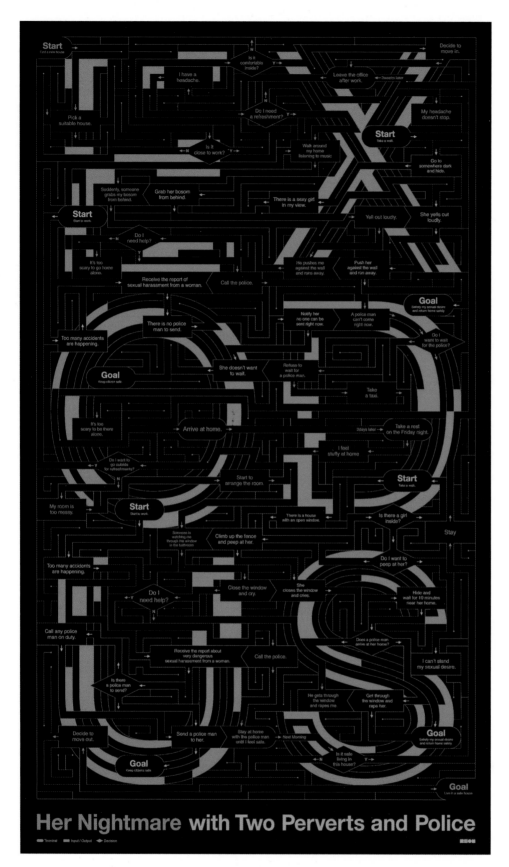

Her Nightmare with Two Perverts and Police

EXODUS
SCHOOL OF THE ART INSTITUTE
OF CHICAGO
DESIGN | Poster Design | Typography

CREATIVE DIRECTOR: Beomyoung Sohn
DESIGN DIRECTOR: Beomyoung Sohn
DESIGNER: Beomyoung Sohn
ILLUSTRATOR: Beomyoung Sohn
COUNTRY: United States

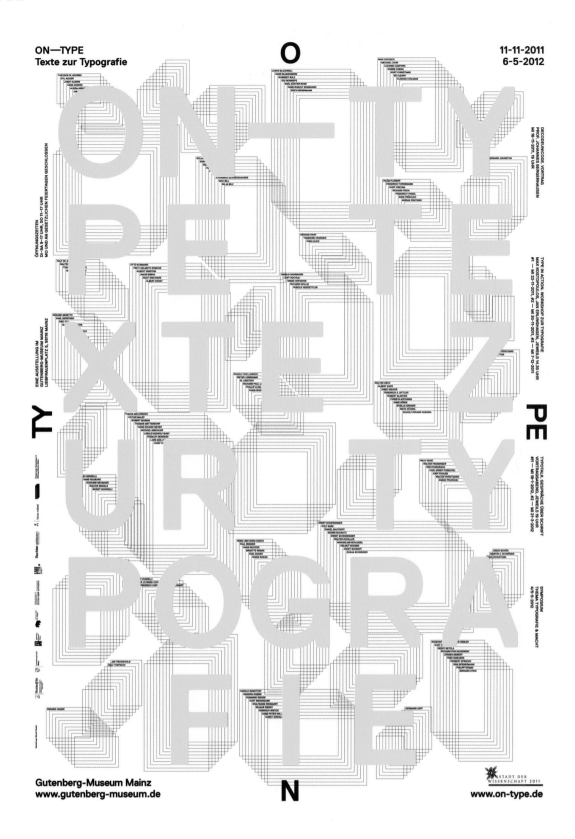

ON-TYPE: TEXTE ZUR TYPOGRAFIE
FH MAINZ UNIVERSITY OF
APPLIED SCIENCES
DESIGN | Poster Design | Typography

DESIGNER: Marcel Häusler
PROJECT MANAGER:
Professor Dr. Isabel Naegele-Spamer,
Professor Dr. Petra Eisele
CLIENT: Gutenberg-Museum Mainz
COUNTRY: Germany

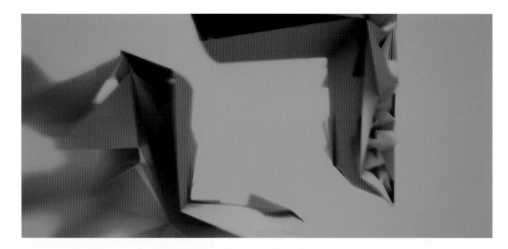

PLAYSTATION
SCHOOL OF VISUAL ARTS
MOTION | Animated Logo

DESIGNER: Adam Grabowski
ANIMATOR: Adam Grabowski
SOUND DESIGN: Joe Johnson
CLIENT: Playstation
COUNTRY: United States

AWAKENING
ART CENTER COLLEGE OF DESIGN
MOTION | Special Effects

DESIGNER: Doug Chang
PHOTOGRAPHER: Mike Reyes, Filippo Nesci,
Clair Chang
DIRECTOR: Doug Chang
VISUAL EFFECTS: Doug Chang
SOUND DESIGN: Doug Chang
COUNTRY: United States

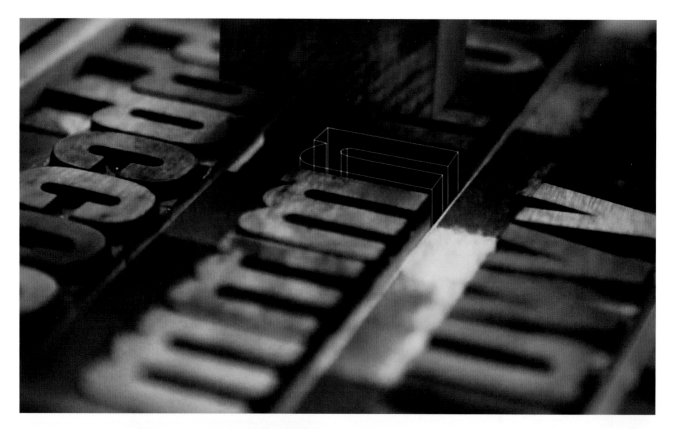

LETTERPRESS
SCHOOL OF VISUAL ARTS
MOTION | Typography

CHAIRMAN: Richard Wilde
CREATIVE DIRECTOR: Naomie Ross
CLIENT: School of Visual Arts
COUNTRY: United States

HELIUM-FILLED BALLOONS DESIGNED LIKE BLOOD-BAGS ARE DISTRIBUTED TO ENCOURAGE BLOOD DONATION

AMERICAN RED CROSS BALLOON
SCHOOL OF VISUAL ARTS
ADVERTISING | Collateral | Promotional

CHAIRMAN: Richard Wilde
CREATIVE DIRECTOR: Frank Anselmo
ART DIRECTOR: Jae Sung Jung, Bomi Jo,
Dahee Song, Manuel Aleman
COPYWRITER: Jae Sung Jung, Bomi Jo,
Dahee Song, Manuel Aleman
CLIENT: American Red Cross
COUNTRY: United States

MINI COOPERS PAINTED IN THE CLASSIC PAINT-BY-NUMBERS STYLE ARE PARKED IN HIGH-TRAFFIC LOCATIONS TO DEMONSTRATE THE COUNTLESS CUSTOMIZATION OPTIONS THAT MINI HAS AVAILABLE.

MINI PAINT BY NUMBERS
SCHOOL OF VISUAL ARTS
ADVERTISING | Ambient/Environmental
Large Scale

CHAIRMAN: Richard Wilde
CREATIVE DIRECTOR: Frank Anselmo
ART DIRECTOR: Nikolai Shorr, Chung Woo Lee,
Bona Jeong
COPYWRITER: Raúl Cosculluela, Gue Rim Lee,
HyoJoo Kim
CLIENT: MINI
COUNTRY: United States

SUSPENSION
CREATIVE CIRCUS
PHOTOGRAPHY | Magazine Editorial
Miscellaneous

PHOTOGRAPHER: Christian Torres
COUNTRY: United States

STATE OF THE WORLD
ANNUAL REPORT
SCHOOL OF VISUAL ARTS
ILLUSTRATION | Corporate/Institutional

ILLUSTRATOR: Petra Velíšková
COUNTRY: United States

OFFICE SPACE – TITLE SEQUENCE
UNIVERSITY OF CINCINNATI
MOTION | Title Design

DESIGNER: Tyler Brooks
ANIMATOR: Tyler Brooks
CLIENT: University of Cincinnati
COUNTRY: United States

office
space

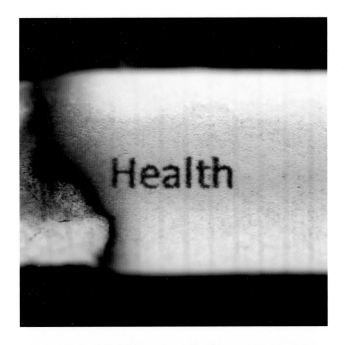

STOP SMOKING
SCHOOL OF VISUAL ARTS
MOTION | Direction

CHAIRMAN: Richard Wilde
CREATIVE DIRECTOR: Jihwan Kim
CLIENT: School of Visual Arts
COUNTRY: United States

PERSONALITY ECLIPSE
SCHOOL OF VISUAL ARTS
MOTION | Cinematography

CHAIRMAN: Richard Wilde
CREATIVE DIRECTOR: Adam Grabowski
CLIENT: School of Visual Arts
COUNTRY: United States

FEDEX PUZZLE BOXES
SCHOOL OF VISUAL ARTS
ADVERTISING | Collateral | Promotional

CHAIRMAN: Richard Wilde
CREATIVE DIRECTOR: Frank Anselmo
ART DIRECTOR: Eleni Georgeou, Scott Steidl
COPYWRITER: Scott Steidl, Eleni Georgeou
CLIENT: FedEx
COUNTRY: United States

Student
Merits

8 BALLOONS
ART CENTER COLLEGE OF DESIGN
MOTION | Direction

CREATIVE DIRECTOR: Kaan Atilla
ART DIRECTOR: Gyum Heo, Jeff Han,
Micael Klok, Ivan Cruz, James Kim
DESIGNER: Gyum Heo, Jeff Han, Micael Klok,
Ivan Cruz, James Kim
ANIMATOR: Gyum Heo, Jeff Han, Micael Klok,
Ivan Cruz, James Kim
COUNTRY: United States

ARTIST PROMOTION
SCHOOL OF VISUAL ARTS
MOTION | Motion Graphics

CHAIRMAN: Richard Wilde
CREATIVE DIRECTOR: Haemin Lim
CLIENT: School of Visual Arts
COUNTRY: United States

**COALITION TO END VIOLENCE
AGAINST WOMEN**
SCHOOL OF VISUAL ARTS
ADVERTISING | Press |
Magazine Consumer Advertisement

CHAIRMAN: Richard Wilde
CREATIVE DIRECTOR: Camilo Galofre,
MyTran Dang
CLIENT: CEVAW
COUNTRY: United States

BLUE COLLAR CRAFT
YORK UNIVERSITY,
SHERIDAN COLLEGE
DESIGN | Book Design |
Image Driven Book

DESIGNER: Man Greig Farin
PHOTOGRAPHER: Man Greig Farin
COUNTRY: Canada

CHILI OIL PORTRAIT
TAMA ART UNIVERSITY
DESIGN | Poster Design | Promotional

CREATIVE DIRECTOR: Hiroki Yamamoto
ART DIRECTOR: Satoshi Kohno
DESIGNER: Satoshi Kohno
PHOTOGRAPHER: Satoshi Kohno
COUNTRY: Japan

KATYA'S ARMOIRE
SCHOOL OF VISUAL ARTS
ILLUSTRATION | Self-Promotion

DESIGNER: Haejeon Jessica Lee
ILLUSTRATOR: Haejeon Jessica Lee
CLIENT: School of Visual Arts
COUNTRY: United States

**PLEASE, SAVE THE DYING
POLAR ANIMAL**
KUNKUK UNIVERSITY
ADVERTISING |
Ambient/Environmental | Small Scale

CHAIRMAN: Ik-hwan Choi
VICE CHAIRMAN: Eun-jin Kwon
EXECTUIVE CREATIVE DIRECTOR: Ik-hwan Choi
CHIEF CREATIVE OFFCIER: Eun-jin Kwon
CREATIVE DIRECTOR: Ik-hwan Choi
DESIGN DIRECTOR: Ik-hwan Choi
SENIOR ART DIRECTOR: Ik-hwan Choi
ART DIRECTOR: Ik-hwan Choi
COPYWRITER: Eun-jin Kwon
COPY EDITOR: Eun-jin Kwon
DESIGNER: Ik-hwan Choi
ILLUSTRATOR: Ik-hwan Choi
HEAD OF PRODUCTION: Eun-jin Kwon
PRODUCTION COMPANY: RealCompany
AGENCY: RealCompany
CLIENT: WWF
COUNTRY: Republic of Korea

ADC Traveling Exhibition

Following the intense period of presentation and jury deliberation, the winning work from each year's Annual Awards is sent off on the Traveling Exhibition. The Exhibition spreads the Art Directors Club's mission to "Connect, Provoke, and Elevate" around the globe, and is the ADC's way of showcasing some of the best pieces done by seasoned professionals and burgeoning new talent on a worldwide scale. It is wonderful to witness the personal connections and reactions to this show, which highlights the best in bold, innovative and creative work.

The Exhibition is hosted at a wide spectrum of institutions, ranging from universities, where students can have their first encounter with the ADC, to renowned agencies where creative professionals can view the work of their peers. It is a privilege for the ADC to partner with these organizations.

The Exhibition spreads
the Art Directors Club's
mission to "Connect,
Provoke, and Elevate"
around the globe.

The Art Directors Club's representative program is in its third year and has
sought out individuals or organizations on an international scale engaged
in Advertising, Design, Interactive/Digital Arts, Photography, Illustration,
Education and Communications, that will help promote global awareness of
the Club as well as the prestige of winning an ADC Cube. The program offers
representatives a unique and rewarding opportunity to be an integral part of
the continued global success of the ADC.

ADC representatives are instrumental in a number of areas: finding hosts for
the annual traveling exhibition; suggesting key individuals to participate on
the jury panel for the Annual Awards Competition; acting as ADC's official
representative in his/her country by distributing ADC press and Annual
Awards information; and helping ADC connect with the advertising, design,
education and visual communications industry in his/her country.

ADC Administration

IGNACIO OREAMUNO
Executive Director

OLGA GRISAITIS
Director of Operations

BRIANNA GRAVES
Director of Communication and
Content

JEN LARKIN KUZLER
Director of Awards Programs

BRENDAN WATSON
Director of Education

KIMBERLY HANZICH
Information Manager

NATHANIEL SALGUEIRO
Design & Content Manager

BRETT MCKENZIE
Content Producer

ZACK KINSLOW
Creative Producer

SARAH WEST
Global Manager, Portfolio Night

ZE MACFARLAND
Director, TOMORROW Awards

**CONOR SHILLEN AND
COLLEN DOYLE,**
One Forest Films
Production Team

HUGO VERDEGUER
Facility Associate

ARIEL ADKINS
Membership Associate

MEREDITH FEIR
Awards Associate

ARIANE HERRERA
PR for the Art Directors Club

**ADC BOARD OF
DIRECTORS**

BENJAMIN PALMER
President
the barbarian group
Co-Founder, Chief Executive Officer

ANTHONY P. RHODES
First Vice President
School of Visual Arts
Executive Vice President

DOUG JAEGER
Advisory Board President
Second Vice President
JaegerSloan Inc.
Partner

CRAIG DUBITSKY
Treasurer
Kind
Managing Partner

ANN HARAKAWA
Secretary
Two Twelve Associates
Principal, Creative Director

STEVE SMITH
Assistant Secretary/
Treasurer
Stephen M. Smith & Co.
Partner

SCOTT BELSKY
Behance LLC
Founder, Chief Executive Officer

BRIAN COLLINS
Collins
Chairman, Chief Creative Officer

ROB FEAKINS
Publicis Kaplan Thaler, New York
President, Chief Creative Officer

JANET FROELICH
Real Simple
Creative Director

REI INAMOTO
AKQA
Chief Creative Officer

NICOLE JACEK
karlssonwilker
Creative Director

RICK KURNIT
Frankfurt, Kurnit & Selz
Partner

ALESSANDRA LARIU
SheSays
Co-Founder

DANY LENNON
The Creative Register Inc.
Owner, President

NOREEN MORIOKA
AdamsMorioka
Partner

CHEE PEARLMAN
Chee Company
Principal

ROB RASMUSSEN
TRIBAL DDB Worldwide
US Chief Creative Officer,
NY Executive Creative Director

JAKOB TROLLBÄCK
Trollbäck and Company
President, Creative Director

ROBERT WONG
Google Creative Lab
Executive Creative Director

Richard J. Walsh 1920-1921
Joseph Chapin 1921-1922
Heyworth Campbell 1922-1923
Fred Suhr 1923-1924
Nathaniel Pousette-Dart 1924-1925
Walter Whitehead 1925-1926
Pierce Johnson 1926-1927

Arthur Munn 1927-1928
Stuart Campbell 1929-1930
Guy Gayler Clark 1930-1931
Edward F. Molyneux 1931-1933
Gordon C. Aymar 1933-1934
Mehemed Fehmy Agha 1934-1935
Joseph Platt 1935-1936
Deane Uptegrove 1936-1938
Walter B. Geoghegan 1938-1940
Lester Jay Loh 1940-1941
Loren B. Stone 1941-1942
William A. Adriance 1942-1943
William A. Irwin 1943-1945
Arthur Hawkins 1945-1946
Paul Smith 1946-1948
Lester Rondell 1948-1950
Harry O'Brien 1950-1951
Roy W. Tillotson 1951-1953
John Jamison 1953-1954
Julian Archer 1954-1955
Frank Baker 1955-1956
William Buckley 1956-1957
Walter R. Grotz 1957-1958
Garret P. Orr 1958-1960
Robert H. Blattner 1960-1961
Edward B. Graham 1961-1962
Bert W. Littman 1962-1964
Robert Sherrich Smith 1964-1965
John A. Skidmore 1965-1967
John Peter 1967-1969
William P. Brockmeier 1969-1971
George Lois 1971-1973
Herbert Lubalin 1973-1974
Louis Dorfsman 1974-1975
Eileen Hedy Schultz 1975-1977
David Davidian 1977-1979
William Taubin 1979-1981
Walter Kaprielian 1981-1983
Andrew Kner 1983-1985
Ed Brodsky 1985-1987
Karl Steinbrenner 1987-1989
Henry Wolf 1989-1991
Kurt Haiman 1991-1993
Allan Beaver 1993-1995
Bill Oberlander 1997-2000
Richard Wilde 2000-2002
Robert Greenberg 2002-2005
Paul Lavoie 2005-2008
Doug Jaeger 2008-2011

DESIGN PARTNER: **DDB°**

91st ANNUAL AWARDS SPONSORS

 Adobe sappi Mother Tongue Writers   bravedog award entry services   Autodesk FLAGSHIP Innovate | Print | Distribute

ADC Members

Gold Corporate Members

Brave Dog
Canon Business Solutions Inc.
Flagship Press
Leo Burnett Worldwide

Silver Corporate Members

72andsunny
Iggesund Paperboard

Corporate Members

the barbarian group
Condé Nast
Frankfurt, Kurnit, Klein & Selz
The Partners
Pentagram Design
Publicis

Academic Members

The Creative Circus
School of Visual Arts

Individual Members

United States

Donna Abbate
Leif Abraham
Gaylord Adams
Roanne Adams
Peter Adler
Charles S. Adorney
Mimmi Ahlberg-Samsel
Jonas Ahlen
Shigeto Akiyama
Senongo Akpem
Craig Allen
Chad Altemose
Erik Altman
Braulio Amado
Jinhee An
Aaryn Anderson
Gail Anderson
Jack Anderson
Gennaro Andreozzi
Jill Andresevic
Kieran Antill
Evan Applegate

Philip Arias
Marc Armato
Inbal Austern
Jordan Awan
Ronald Bacsa
Priscilla Baer
Elizabeth Baldwin
Nancy Balsamello
Dan Balser
Don Barron
Robert Barthelmes
Jonathan Bartlett
Liz Bauer
Allan Beaver
Rodger Belknap
Shannon Bellanca
Scott Belsky
Heidi Berg
John Berg
Barbara Berger
Francesco Bertocci
Candace Bexell-Oukacine
Michael Bierut
Daniel Blackman
Nicholas Blechman
Robert H. Blend
Andrew Boal
Tom Bodkin
Nikki Bodnar
Nina Boesch
John Boiler
Thomas Bonnin
Joseph Botero
Parker Bowab
Conor Brady
Monica Brand
Elisa Breuer-Penello
David Bridges
Ed Brodsky
Ruth Brody
Wilson Brown
Bruno E. Brugnatelli
Greg Brunkalla
Derek Brusin
Dora Budor
Sandra Burch
Mikey Burton
Jordan Butcher
Kristen Cahill
Marsha Camera
Bernard Canniffe
Wilson Capellan
Carlos Cardozo
Thomas Carnase
Mike Carsten
Luis Casamayor
Michelle Casanova
Jon Cassill
Diana Catherines
Katia Cerwin

Anthony Chaplinsky Jr.
Elody Chappuy
Sy-Jenq Cheng
Ivan Chermayeff
Aaron Chiesa
Yon Joo Choi
Rama Chorpash
Mary Choueiter
Fusako Chubachi
Shelly Chung
Stanley Church
Seymour Chwast
Tana Cieciora
Rachel Cirone
Amy Citron
Thomas F. Clemente
Joann Coates
Jacob Cohen
Paul Cohen
Alison Colby
Brian Collins
Steve Colon
Justin Cone
Fiona Conrad
Jon Contino
Wade Convay
Robert Cooney
Andrew Coppa
John Cornette
Alison Cornyn
Rodrigo Corral
Andres Cortes
Brent Couchman
Bernadette Coughlin
Niko Courtelis
Nick Couts
John Cowell
Lindsay Craig
Meg Crane
Susan Credle
Kathleen Creighton
Darrin Crescenzi
Maja Cule
Alison Curry
Sara Cwynar
Keith D'Mello
Jennifer Daniel
Flory Danish
Jakob Daschek
David Davidian
Dominic Davidson-Merritt
Gabe Davis
Myrna Davis
Randi B. Davis
Jessica Dawson
Luca De Rosso
Mario de Toledo-Sader
Stuart deHaan
Joe Del Sorbo
Michala Dening

Richard DeSimone
Joseph DiGioia
Brian DiLorenzo
Jacquelyn DiStaulo
Jason Dodd
Edward Donald
Jaclyn Dooner
Gal Dor
Marc Dorian
Kay E. Douglas
Craig Dubitsky
Aaron Duffy
Donald H. Duffy
Kim Dulaney
Arem Duplessis
Gautam Dutta
Bailey Dwyer
Tom Dzolan
Ken Edge
Jai-Lee Egna
Stanley Eisenman
Alexander Eissing
Joseph Ellis
Luis Enriquez
Lee Epstein
Janet Esquirol
Ximena Etchart
Corinna Falusi
Tayef Farrar
Rob Feakins
Jeffrey Felmus
Karen Finckenor
Hunter Fine
Mikell Fine Iles
Colleen Finn
Blanche Fiorenza
Carl Fischer
Georg Fischer
Rochelle Fisher
Vanessa Fortier
Lui Francisco
Stephen Frankfurt
Christina Freyss
Sabrina Friebis-Ruiz
Janet Froelich
Ada Fung
Yoko Furusho
Croix Gagnon
Sean Gallagher
Danielle Gallo
Brian Ganton Jr.
Lucas García de Polavieja
Gino Garlanda
Steff Geissbuhler
John Gellos
Eleni Georgeou
Michael Gericke
Steven Gilliatt
Frank C. Ginsberg
Bob Giraldi

Steve Giralt
Milton Glaser
Julie Glassberg
Rachel Gogel
Bill Gold
Priscilla Gomez
Ana Gomez Bernaus
Scott Goodman
Michele Gorham
Shaun Gough
Carly Grafstein
Ray Graj
Francesca Grassi
Michael Greenberg
Norm Grey
Jack Griffin
Glenn Groglio
Raisa Grubshteyn
Adalberto Guedes Santana
Mariam Guessous
Peter Gunther
David Haan
Jordan Hadley
Frank Hahn
Kurt Haiman
Laurent Hainaut
Allan Haley
David Hand
Ann Harakawa
Tim Harms
Jaz Harold
Simon Harsent
Hollis Hart
Keith Hart
Steve Haslip
Brad Hasse
Luke Hayman
Alexander Heil
David Hermanas
Nancy Herrmann
Bobby Hershfield
Elana Hershman
Toni Hess
Jennifer Heuer
Andy Hirsch
Joshua Hirsch
Marilyn Hoffner
Joel Holland
Holly Holliday
Alex Holt-Cohan
Jin-Hyuk Hong
Uajit Hongkiatkhajorn
Andrew S. Hoydich
Cavan Huang
Bradley Hughes
Elisabetta Iannucci
Rei Inamoto
Todd Irwin
Raisa Ivannikova
Zeynab Izadyar
Nicole Jacek
Harry Jacobs
Carlos Jadraque
Doug Jaeger
David Jalbert-Gagnier
John Jay
Colin Jeffery

Joe Johnson
Lars Jorgensen
Leo Jung
Ardis Kadiu
Lilit Kalachyan
Jun Ku Kang
Jaï Kapadia
Walter Kaprielian
Emilie Kareh
Scott Keglovic
Dan Kenneally
Dogyun Kim
Elle Jeong Eun Kim
Hoon Kim
Jisun Kim
Sunghee Kim
Sungwook Kim
Yoni Kim
Jacquelyn Kirby
Marc Klatzko
Judith Klein
Hilda Stanger Klyde
Andrew Kner
Tomas Kohoutek
Ali Kohut
Andrew Kornhaber
Jean-Francois Kowalski
Stephen Krill
Rick Kurnit
Ari Kuschnir
Jin Hee Kwon
Dan LaCivita
Roni Lagin
Natalie Lam
Brad Lande
Katelyn Lanphier
Anthony LaPetri
Leonardo Lawson
Sal Lazzarotti
Jeff Leaf
Eric Lee
Gina Lee
Hyesu Lee
Michael Lee
Travis Lee
Young Lim Lee
Audrey Lefevre
Dany Lennon
Mitch Lenzen
Tisa Lerner
Veronika Levin
Rachel Levine
Tamar Levine
Micah Lidberg
Rodrigo Lino Gonzalez
Jeremy Lips
Jen Little
Rebecca Lloyd
George Lois
Antonio Lopez
Rodrigo Lopez
Thomas Losinski
Roman Luba
Matthew Luckhurst
Martinez Miranda Luis
Laura Lutz
Richard MacFarlane

David H. MacInnes
Michael MacNeill
Patrick Macomber
Lou Magnani
Pablo Maldonado
John Malone
Gregory Malphurs
Kristin Manning
Alex Mapar
Leo J. Marino, III
Jackson Mariucci
Bobby Martin
Gina Martynova
Joseph Masci
Jamie Massam
William McCaffery
J. Mason McFee
Scott Meola
Chris Merriam
Trevor Messersmith
Victoria Messner
Jackie Merri Meyer
Abbott Miller
Tomasz Modzelewski
Hsiang Chin Moe
Yuen Ki Mok
Andrew Montague
Ross Moody
Thomas Mori
Noreen Morioka
Haydn Morris
Oliver Munday
Leigh Munro
Yoshichika Murakami
Elizabeth Nanut
Jessica Natches
Chris Silas Neal
Joel Nealy
Julia Neiva
Jose Jorge Netto
Lauren Niebes
Courtney Nienke
Joseph Nissen
David November
Mehera O'Brien
Husani Oakley
Nak Kyu Oh
John Okladek
Chelsea Oliver
Emilie Olsson
Nick Onken
Karin Onsager-Birch
Eddie Opara
Lysa Opfer
Catherine Orriss
Ana Maria Osorio
Ricardo Ovelar
Onofrio Paccione
Aaron Padin
Benjamin Palmer
Lauren Panepinto
Cynthia Park
Joo Young Park
Youngjun Park
Marcel Parrilla
Karyn Pascoe
John Passafiume

Christiane Paul
Chee Pearlman
Joshua Pereira
Robert Perino
Harold A. Perry
Robert Petrocelli
Scott Petts
Theodore D. Pettus
Allan A. Philiba
Brad Phillips
Frederico Phillips
Jessica Philpott
Alma Phipps
Eric Pike
Tanguy Pinte
Ernest Pioppo
Larry Pipitone
Carlos Pisco
Cory Pitzer
Robert Pliskin
Kira Pollack
Kenton Powell
Neil Powell
Shelly Prisella
Ana Racelis
Luis Ramos
Robert Rasmussen
Unnikrishnan Raveendranathen
Samuel Reed
Emma Reichert
Herbert Reinke
Kimberly Rhee
Anthony Rhodes
David Rhodes
Stan Richards
Jason Ring
J Matthew Riva
Klajdi Robo
Luis Roca
Jason Rockwood
Odoardo Rodriguez
Jungyeon Roh
Andy Romano
Heather Rosen
Glenn Rosko
Charlie Rosner
John Rothenberg
Michael Roznowski
Jaron Rubenstein
Renee Rupcich
Don Ruther
Stephen Rutterford
Leen Sadder
Fitgi Saint-Louis
Satoru Saito
Robert Saks
Gillian Salit
Robert Salpeter
Krista Samoles
Benjamin Sandler
Stanton Sarjeant
Sam Scali
Ernest Scarfone
Anthony Scerri
Michael Schachtner
Marc Scheff
Daniel Scheibel

Paula Scher
David Schimmel
Karen Schnelwar
Harry Schnitzler
Chris Schoenman
Eileen Hedy Schultz
Jacob Schwartz
Birgit Schwarz-Hickey
Anthony Scumaci
William Seabrook, III
Leslie Segal
Rachel Segal
Sheldon Seidler
Danny Shaw
Thomas (Dong Hwi) Shim
Michael Shirley
Joe Shouldice
Bonnie Siegler
Bulent Sik
Piotr Sikora
Milton Simpson
Sheilini Singh
Leonard Sirowitz
Ron Sizemore
Kristina Slade
Kristin Sloan
Aamir Smith
John Smith
Phil Smith
Virginia Smith
Stephanie Sobel Lobron
Gerardo Somoza
Gerald Soto
Nicole Spiegel-Gotsch
Darren Spiller
Chad Springer
Joe Staluppi
Mindy Phelps Stanton
Matteo Stanzani
Karl Steinbrenner
Fernanda Steinmann
Peter Stemmler
Eric Stevens
Jimmie Stone
Rob Strasberg
Greg Strelecki
Andre Stringer
William Strosahl
Michelle Sukle
Orion Tait
Yasui Takehiko
James Talerico
Dana Tanamachi
Simone Tarantino
Persia Tatar
Miesha Tate
Graham Taylor
Robert Taylor
Mark Tekushan
Justin Ternullo
Mariano Testa
Richard The
Ramon Thompson
Oscar Tillman
Siung Tjia
Georgia Tribuiani
Ling Tsui

Rich Tu
Tracy Turner
Mark Tutssel
Yuichi Uchida
Tomi Um
Markus Vaga
Jim Van Hise
Diane Painter Velletri
Claudio Venturini
Ronaldo Vianna
Stephen Viksjo
Domenico Vitale
Scott Vitrone
Andrew Vucinich
Michael J. Walsh Jr.
Kevin Wang
Barbara Warnke
Mike Wasilewski
Gavin Wassung
Steve Wax
Jessica Weber
Jay Wedin
Susan Weil
Roy Weinstein
Ari Weiss
Mark Wenneker
Elias Wessel
Robert Shaw West
James Widegren
Ariel Wilchek
Richard Wilde
Lee Wilson
Piera Wolf
Laury Wolfe
Robert Wong
Willy Wong
Martin Wonnacott
Wanju Wu
Faris Yakob
James Kyungmo Yang
Nate Yates
Iee Ling Yee
Chieh Yen
You Jung Yoon
Burton Yount
JungIn Yun
Juleah Zach
Anthony Zambataro
Mark Zapico
Gabriella Zappia
Linling Zha
Bernie Zlotnick
Alan H. Zwiebel
kHyal

Argentina

Camilo Barria Royer
Horacio Lorente
Valeria Pesqueira
Guillermo Tragant

Australia

Sian Binder
Kellie Campbell-Illingworth
Tim Flattery

Matt Huynh
Madeleine Mary

Austria

Mariusz Jan Demner
Franz Merlicek

Brazil

Joao Carlos Mosterio
Guillermo Vega
Renata Zincone

Canada

Philippe Archontakis
George Argyropoulos
Christian Ayotte
Brian Banton
Toby Bartlett
Israel Bonequi
Rob Carter
Audrey Chiarelli
Siew Ling Chow
Ryan Crouchman
Marta Cutler
Louis Gagnon
Juan Madrigal
Homer Mendoza
Kevin Peacock
Steve Persico
Ric Riordon
Genevieve Simms
Dominique Trudeau
Rupesh Vetha

China

Li Chaosheng
Jiaying Han
Lin Jingyang
Kelvin Qu
Zhou Wenjun
Hei Yiyang
Daolin Zhao

Colombia

Sebastian Barbosa

Croatia

Marko Korzinek

Denmark

Thomas Petersen
Andreas Rasmussen

Finland

Inka Järvinen

France

Richard Cohen

Jeremie Fontana
Romain Guichard
Nicolas Jacquette
Mat Letellier

Germany

Stefan Becker
Michael Eibes
Tina Glahr
Harald Haas
Sascha Hanke
Oliver Hesse
Michael Hoinkes
Saskia Ketz
Christoph Kirst
Claus Koch
Oliver Krippahl
Andreas Lueck
Joel Micah Miller
Efstathios Minokoglou
Rene Natzel
Malte Reidenbach
Achim Riedel
Sven Ruhs
Vesa Sammalisto
Jens Schmidt
Tristan Schmitz
Joerg Schneider
Klaus Trommer
Mathias Vietmeier
Oliver Weiss
Luo Yu
Joerg Zuber

Greece

John Magas
Rodanthi Senduka

Hong Kong

David Au
David Chow
Keith Ho

Iran

Naghmeh Felor Zabihi

Israel

Kobi Barki
Igor Ginzburg

Italy

Alberto Baccari
Sam Baron
Jonathan Calugi
Andrea Castelletti
Moreno Chiacchiera
Dario Curatolo
Alessandro Demicheli
Pasquale Diaferia
Davide Fissore
Federigo Gabellieri

Debora Manetti
Cristina Marcellini
Lorenzo Marini
Claudia Neri
Roberto Ottolino
Giorgio Stefano Rocco
Camilla Venturini

Japan

Norio Fujishiro
Motoko Hada
Takahisa Hashimoto
Keiko Hirata
Seiichi Hishikawa
Tomoyuki Hishiya
Kohei Horiuchi
Kogo Inoue
Mitsuyuki Ishibashi
Yoshichika Ishibashi
Keiko Itakura
Genki Ito
Yasuyuki Ito
Akira Kagami
Takeshi Kagawa
Seijo Kawaguchi
Akiko Kuze
Manabu Mizuno
Kentaro Nagai
Norikazu Nakamura
Shingo Noma
Sadanori Nomura
Yoshimi Oba
Kuniyasu Obata
Yasumichi Oka
Hiroshi Saito
Michihito Sasaki
Akira Sato
Kenichiro Shigetomi
Yutaka Takahama
Katsumi Tamura
Soji George Tanaka
Yasuo Tanaka
Katsunori Watanabe
Yoshiko Watanabe
Akihiro H. Yamamoto
Yoji Yamamoto
Masaru Yokoi
Syoh Yoshida

Kazakhstan

Juan Pablo Valencia

Republic of Korea

Kwang Kyu Kim
Taelin Oh
Kum-jun Park

Mexico

Miguel Calderon
Luis Ramirez

Netherlands

Irma Boom

New Zealand

Andy Blood
Clem Devine

Nigeria

Oluseyi Frederick-Wey
Nduka Kade

Norway

Randi Aardal
Jens Benneche

Philippines

Teddy Catuira

Russia

Alexey Fadeyev
Alexey Malina

Serbia

Nenad Karadjinovic
Rade Šaptovic

Singapore

Felix Ng
Hal Suzuki
Yah-Leng Yu

Slovenia

Eduard Cehovin

Spain

Juan Astasio
Jaime Beltran
Ena Cardenal de la Nuez
Belen Coca
Sandra Garcia Pagola
Otilia Martin Gonzalez
Angel Montero Barro
Alexander Trochut

Sweden

Gustav Arnetz
Kari Palmqvist
Martin Ringqvist

Switzerland

Florian Beck
Stephan Bundi
MC Casal
Conrad Malcher
Dominique Anne Schuetz
Philipp Welti

Taiwan

Alain Fa-Hsiang Hu

Thailand

Surachai Puthikulangkura

Turkey

Pinar Barutcu Fricke

United Arab Emirates

Komal Bedi Sohal

United Kingdom

Alessandro Alpago
Kyle Bean
Simon Canaway
Oliver Durant
David Eveleigh-Evans
Owen Gildersleeve
Michael Harrison
Jimmy Lenoir
Sara Pettinella
Malcolm Poynton
Pete Rossi
Benjamin Shrimpton
Ian Wharton
James Wignall
Matthew Willey

Student Groups

Fashion Institute of Technology
Minneapolis College of Art and Design
Pratt Institute
Savannah College of Art & Design

Student Members

Hilman Abdullah
Luke Aiello
Rachel Ake
Najeebah Al-Ghadban
Doug Aldrich
Cecilia Almeida
Brian Anderson
Johnas Andre
Astrid Andujar
Michelle Angelosanto
Cecili Antares
Ben Apatow
Danielle Arbib
Allyson Arboleda
Jared Aucourant
Rodger Austin
Tara Avery
Oluwafemi Awokoya
Saebom Bae

Alexandra Barron
Victoria Bellavia
Alexandra Bey
Edmund Boey
Patrick Boiteau
Justine Brilmyer
Simona Bunardzhieva
Amanda Camodeo
Christian Campbell
Brittany Carter
Nuri Cha
Lisa Champ
Paul Chang
Alan Chao
Gin Chen
Melanie Chernock
Yooln Cho
Steve Choi
Jonas Christiansen
Jailee Chung
Jayeon Chung
Noelle Clark
Jeff Close
Bryan Coello
Joey Cofone
Lindsey Cole
Alyssa Colina
Andrew Collette
Michelle Constant
Kristen Corna
Kathryn Corning
Michael Costa
Lisa Cracchiolo
James Czyz
Kelli Daly
MyTran Dang
Yuri Darius
Nicole David
Bryan Davis
Mary Day
Jocelyn de Almeida
Danielle De Biasio
Vidya Deepak
Alisha Denomme
Tom Dickson
Elisabetta Distefano
Olga Domoradova
Elizabeth Doyle
Julie Doyle
Megan Drennan
Nina Dubin
Lyanne Dubon
Nora Elbaz
Natalie Encalada
Julia Endow
Sophie Erskine
John Espina
Samantha Evers
Michael Falco
Jin Fan
Ladi Fatade
Rachel Feldman
Doda Ferrari
Aileen Ferris
Ryan Fitzgerald
Kim Foster
Camilo Galofre

Jessie Gang
Myles Gaythwaite
Ross Gendels
Ryan Goldberg
Kayla Gomez
Daniel Gonzalez
Vera Gorbunova
Marie Graboso
Jacob Grady
Ben Grandgenett
Hayley Grassetti
Rachel Greene
Tamas Greguricz
Alban Grosdidier
Nigel Gross
Deborah Gruber
Adam Hada
Emily Hale
Hunter Hampton
Kári Emil Helgason
Thinne Helleskov
Sooim Heo
Shannon Hicks
Schuyler Higgins
Spencer Hill
Abby Hirsh
Erina Ho
Yuwei Ho
Lauren Hom
Tiffany Hong
Katherine Honig
Kat Hornstein
Nazmul Howlader
Longpeng Huang
Shih-Ying Hung
Aimee Hunt
Christine Hunt
YooJung Hwang
Jeffrey Iacoboni
Tara Iannotti
Grace Ilori
Haenara Im
Consuelo Izquierdo
Kyle Janisch
Whittline Jean
Yi-Chieh Jen
Robert Jencks
Bin Jiang
Rochelle Jiang
Malissa Johnson
Miles Johnson
Emma Joslyn
SooJin Jung
Aramazt Kalayjian
Rachel Kaminetzky
Jeong A Kang
Yoojung Kang
Callie Kant
Marina Kawata
Jahanzeb Khan
Jessica Killian
Anna Kim
Christopher Kim
Da On Kim
Ha Lim Kim
Hae In Kim
HaYan Kim

Hyobee Kim
Hyunjin Kim
Ja Young Kim
Janet Kim
Jeong Yun Kim
JeongWoo Kim
Ji Won Kim
Jinkyoung Kim
Joung Soo Kim
Minah Kim
Minsun Kim
Moonjung Kim
Sin Young Kim
Won Young Kim
Woonji Kim
Yeon Hee Kim
Yoon Hee Kim
Young wook Kim
Ian Kirk
Jilly Ko
Taeyoun Ko
Dominika Kramerova
Sherry Hsin-Ting Kuo
Michael Kushner
Donna Kwon
Margot Laborde
Brianna Laurice
Anna Laytham
Ella Laytham
Donna Lee
Elle Euikyung Lee
Gary Lee
Jaedon Lee
Jennifer Lee
Jenny Lee
Ji Soo Lee
Jisol Lee
Su Yeon Lee
Yong Jun Lee
Yoonji Lee
Yu Jin Lee
Stephanie Levine
Kathryn Lewis
Suzanne Li
Carina Liebmann
Rebecca Lim
Chia Yang Lin
Musen Lin
Kate Ling
Hsinyu Liu
Amanda Lodi
Lisa Lok
Chen Longo
Ekaterina Lopantseva
Neil Lopez
Nina LoSchiavo
Justin Lucey
Stephanie Macchione
Karen Mainenti
Olivia Maramara
Alane Marco
Alfred Marks
Henry Martinez
Jessicya Materano
Garri Matnadze
Emily Matsuno
Sara McCarthy

Bobbi Jo McCauley
Kelly McGreen
Gail McLaurin
Jeffrey Melo
Marvin Menke
Jacopo Miceli
Nia Middleton
Christopher Mills
Sebit Min
Ahyoung Moon
John Moroz
Erin Murphy
Meaghan Murray
Julie Muszynski
Kyung-A Na
Teresa Naranjo
Hamon Nasiri Honarvar
Kyle Nasypany
Christopher Nelson
Jerrod New
Kevin Ng
Laura Ng
Alec Nickell
Dominika Nicman
Julia Norris
Mariam Noureddin
Cheri Nowak
Dan Ogren
Ali Olsen-Beever
Jonathan Ong
Jennifer Oviedo
Melisa Ozkan
Jiangshengyu Pan
Lisa Papa
Deanna Paquette
Candice Park
Chan Young Park
Elaine Park
Guewon Park
Haewon Park
Nari Park
Seongmi Park
Rodrigo Pedreira
Chris Pinter
Brett Pollack
Allison Pottasch
Ryan Potter
Christopher Potts
Andrei Prakurat
Caroline Pratt
Rosie Pringle
Mergime Raci
Oana Radulescu
Robert Raspanti
Kimberley Rebetti
Anthony Reda
Amanda Reilly
Michael Riso
Brittany Rivera
Jessica Rodriguez
Latimel Rodriguez
Leah Romero
Samantha Russo
Elizabeth Sadkowski
Sasha Safir-Temple
Kate Sanders
Josefina Santos

April Scarduzio
Elise Schachter
Hannelore Schaffner
Andrew Seetoh
Emilee Serafine
Kelly Shami
Anna Shausmanova
Emily Shaw
Murray Shaw
Carly Sheehan
Jean Shim
Jarwon Jamie Shin
Tal Shub
Johanna Silfa
Jason Silverman
Jennifer Sims
Dahyeon Dana Sow
Jaiti Srivastava
Minjung Suh
Robin Tagliasacchi
William Tam
Yu Ting Tan
Ren Tarpley
Andrew Teoh
Stephanie Tin
Freddie Torberntsson
Steve Torres
Danielle Tremblay
Holly Trotta
Lynsey Tuthill
Tabitha Ueblacker
Pedro Vega
Ashley Veltre
Bruce Viemeister
Christina Walters
Philipp Weidhofer
Stephen Weisbrot
Rachel Willey
King Chun Wong
Youmin Woo
Mengwen Xiang
Kaz Yamaguchi
Jiyoon Yeom
Erika Yost
Chan Ju Yu
Ester Zar
Adam Zeiner
Edoardo Zenone
Fei Zhong
Zipeng Zhu

Index

Index

Index

Index

Index